Mike the Tiger

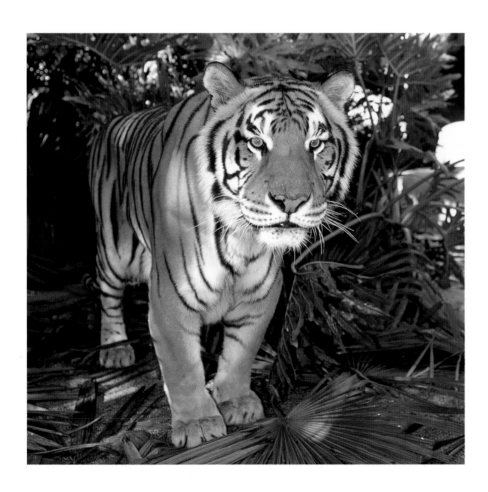

Mike the Tiger

Text by David G. Baker and W. Sheldon Bivin

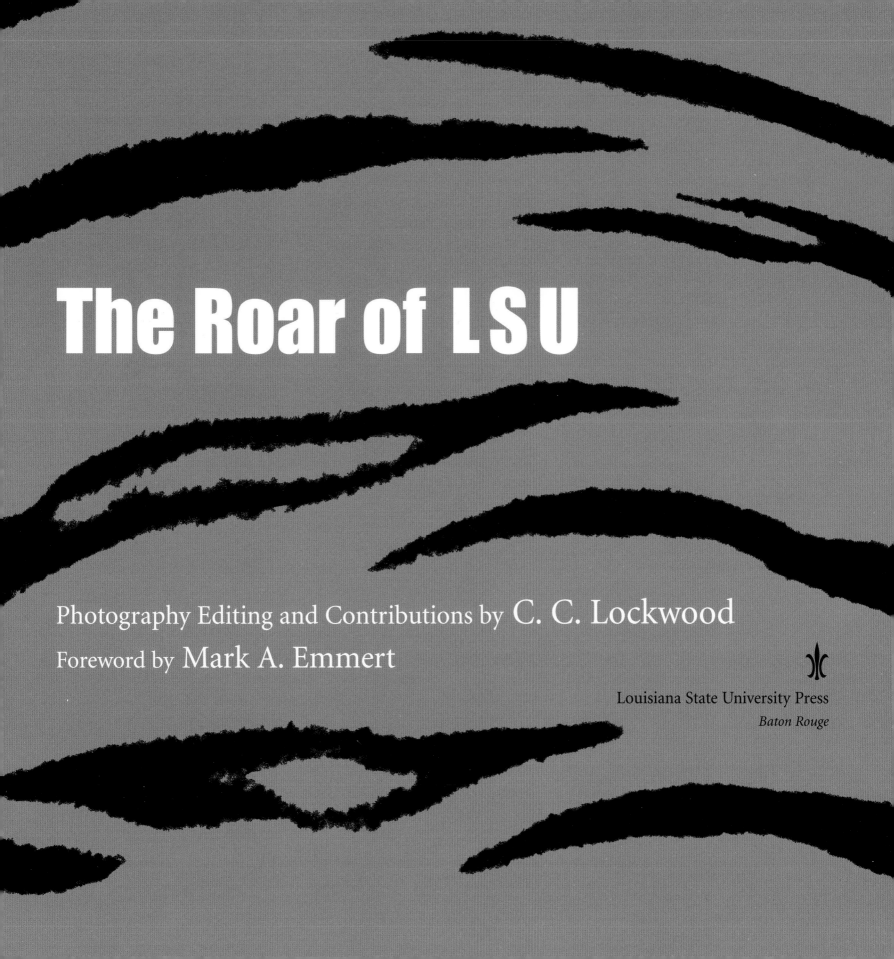

The Roar of LSU

Photography Editing and Contributions by C. C. Lockwood

Foreword by Mark A. Emmert

Louisiana State University Press
Baton Rouge

Manufactured in China
First printing
12   11   10   09   08   07   06   05   04   03
5   4   3   2   1

Designer: Laura Roubique Gleason
Typeface: Minion text with Impact display
Printer and binder: Dai Nippon Printing

Library of Congress Cataloging-in-Publication Data:
Baker, David G., 1956–
    Mike the Tiger : the roar of LSU / text by David G. Baker and
W. Sheldon Bivin ; photography editing and contributions by
C. C. Lockwood ; foreword by Mark A. Emmert.
        p.   cm.
    ISBN 0-8071-2888-0 (pbk. : alk. paper)
    1. Louisiana State University (Baton Rouge, La.) — Mascots
— History. 2. LSU Tigers (Football team) — History. I. Bivin,
W. Sheldon. II. Lockwood, C. C., 1949–   III. Title.
    GV958.L65.B34 2003
    796.332'63'0976318—dc21
                                        2003001651

This book is dedicated to Mrs. De Laine Emmert.
Without her enthusiasm, initiative, and love for LSU and Mike the Tiger,
this book would not have been possible.

Jim Zietz, University Relations

Contents

Foreword *Chancellor Mark A. Emmert*

Mike the Tiger is quintessentially LSU. Innately wise, fiercely competitive, ungrudgingly proud, and ever majestic, in living form Mike represents the enduring character of all people and things LSU. It is thus no surprise that for nearly seventy years he has embodied the spirit and resolve of our great university and has inspired young and old with the wondrous feeling of knowing what it is to be a Tiger.

Mike represents a Fighting Tiger tradition that dates back to the Civil War. The story of our Bengal tiger mascots reveals the unending dedication of innumerable students, faculty, and staff, as well as tremendous community patrons who have cared for and supported the animals since Mike I's first arrival at LSU in 1936. Without doubt, anyone who has ever met "Mike" has his or her own story to tell.

Mike the Tiger: The Roar of LSU brims with such fond remembrances, reminding us of the cunning and wiling ways of Mike I; of the premature demise of Mike II; of Mike III's ability to growl on cue; of Mike IV's unleashed stroll down North Stadium Drive; and of Shaquille O'Neal's frequent visits to see the playful Mike V. The responsibilities of caring for an animal weighing close to five hundred pounds, with all of the medical challenges, travel requirements, movie set demands, and diet needs that come with the role, become wonderfully clear within. So does the vital role LSU students have played over the years in raising the funds to bring several of our Mikes to campus, fending off Tulane pranksters attempting to spray him green, and raising enough ruckus over his arrival on campus to lead university administrators to call an "academic holiday" in Mike's honor.

As James Wharton, chancellor emeritus of LSU, puts it, Mike *is* LSU. Beyond symbolizing the essence of the university and its people, Mike helps LSU fulfill its fundamental role, which is to educate. Attracting more than 100,000 visitors a year, Mike's commanding presence spreads knowledge of the Bengal tiger and increases awareness of the endangerment facing his species. As the university continues striving to provide Mike with the habitat he deserves and in which he can be most comfortable, the educational opportunities Mike affords us will increase exponentially.

Mike the Tiger: The Roar of LSU is for every loyal Tiger fan. It is for those who continue to get goose bumps when they visit Mike outside the Pete Maravich Assembly Center or when they witness his grand parade around Tiger Stadium on a Saturday night in the fall. His history is our history, as is his indomitable spirit.

Geaux Tigers!

Chancellor Mark A. Emmert with the mascot Mike at the homecoming football game in 1999.

Jim Zietz, University Relations

Acknowledgments

Anyone who has been involved in the care of Mike the Tiger over the years knows that it is far more than any one person can do. While the veterinarians are frequently in the limelight, many people behind the scenes deserve heartfelt thanks for the parts they have played in caring for our precious mascots. The student caretakers, most of whom are now doctors of veterinary medicine or other successful professionals, have provided over sixty-five years of outstanding day-to-day care for the tigers. One of our greatest joys has been to observe the change in our student caretakers as the responsibility of caring for Mike molds them into mature, dedicated professionals. Our wives and children also deserve recognition for allowing us time away from home during the many hours we have spent caring for Mike, taking him to various events, and telling his story to audiences of all kinds. Our care of Mike has largely been provided after normal working hours, on our personal time. In addition, as we have each served as Mike's veterinarian, we have been on call twenty-four hours a day, seven days a week. This is a sacrifice for any family.

From the beginning, the Athletic Department has graciously provided most or all of the financial resources for Mike's care. Several people, including Jim Blanchard, Paulette Johnson, John Symank, Al Richard, Bill Perkins, and others, have kept Mike's aging enclosure in working order long after it should have fallen apart or have assisted with other aspects of his care. The LSU Police Department has graciously provided police escort for Mike whenever he leaves the campus. The importance of this service cannot be overstated. When Mike V has required surgery, he has been most vulnerable to serious complications after being injected with anesthetics in his cage. At those times, LSU police officers stopped traffic and provided escort, allowing us to move Mike quickly to the School of Veterinary Medicine, where we could care for him. Dr. Pirie of the Baton Rouge Zoo has been our friend, advisor, and a faithful assisting veterinarian for both Mike IV and Mike V. Doug Guidroz and Rick Vallet of Central Hitch and Equipment generously provided Mike's new traveling trailer, while Troy LeBlanc of Ascension Fleet and Collision Repair Center graciously repainted the trailer free of charge, in the hopes that it will last as long as the previous trailer. What a blessing that trailer has been. When Mike IV or Mike V needed medical care beyond what could be provided inside his enclosure, the faculty and staff of the School of Veterinary Medicine have assisted us in providing the best medical care possible. Without the resources of the veterinary school, it would not be possible to provide such special animals the kind of care they deserve. The animal caretaker staff in the Division of Laboratory Animal Medicine in the School of Veterinary Medicine have moved

caging, repaired doors, and on very short notice, provided many other essential services on Mike's behalf. Mr. Rick Ramsey, assistant director of the Division of Laboratory Animal Medicine, has donated his time and creative abilities to construct a variety of devices that have helped us move and care for the tigers safely. The good people at the Baton Rouge Zoo, under the leadership of directors George Felton and Phil Frost, graciously took Mike IV and Mike V in as guests when additional housing was needed. They cared for them as if they were one of their own. Likewise, Bob Cooper and the staff of the Little Rock Zoo graciously accommodated Mike IV in 1981 while his cage was renovated.

Several people helped make this book possible. Foremost among them was Alison Borchgrevink, our faithful and hardworking student worker who spent hours ferreting out obscure facts and photos and following up on leads for additional information. It would not have been possible for us to accumulate all of this information without Alison's help. We also wish to thank student employee Thomas Todd. We also thank General Ron Richard (USMC, retired) of the Tiger Athletic Foundation for funding Alison and Tom while they researched material for this book. Faye Phillips of the Hill Memorial Library at LSU regularly went the extra mile to provide Alison with useful historical information. We also received tremendous support and assistance from Laura Gleason, Maureen Hewitt, George Roupe, and Les Phillabaum of LSU Press. The high quality of this work is in large part due to their professionalism. Several historically significant photographs were graciously contributed by Jim Amoss and Nancy Burris of the New Orleans *Times-Picayune* and Doug Manship Jr. and Jill Arnold of the Baton Rouge *Advocate.* In addition, many private individuals, including several former LSU student tiger caretakers, their friends, and relatives, came forward with interesting information, anecdotes, and photographs, which they graciously contributed. Special thanks are also due the Lamar Family Foundation, whose generous monetary contribution has helped make this book more affordable to all Mike's fans. Lastly, we are especially appreciative of Jim Zietz and Harry Cowgill, both of whom were very generous with their time and photographic talents. It is these personal touches from so many people that have made this book so special.

We could go on and on. So many people have willingly donated their time and talents to help us care for our beloved mascots. We want to express our sincere thanks and appreciation to each person, named and unnamed. We thank you all.

—David G. Baker, W. Sheldon Bivin, and
C. C. Lockwood

Harry M. Cowgill

Mike the Tiger

A Louisiana Tiger

Courtesy National Archives

The Early Years (1861–1936)

Just how did the LSU student athletes become known as the Tigers? To answer this question we have to go back to a dark period in the history of this great nation. North and South were about to engage in the bloodiest war ever fought on the North American continent. On January 26, 1861, Louisiana seceded from the Union. Civil War appeared imminent. In communities all over Louisiana, companies of soldiers were organized to serve in the Confederate army. One of the first companies formed gave itself the name Tiger Rifles. The Tiger Rifles were under the leadership of Captain Alex White, a veteran of the Mexican War. To say that the Tigers were colorful is not only literally true but an understatement of comical proportions. The battalion had been outfitted with outlandish uniforms similar to those worn by French Zouaves. They wore scarlet skull caps, red shirts, open blue jackets, and baggy blue and white striped pants tucked

These replicas show the colorful uniform worn by the Louisiana Tigers.

Major Chatham Roberdeau
Wheat, C.S.A., commander
of the 1st Louisiana Special
Battalion, which included
the Tiger Rifles.

Courtesy Mrs. William Elam

served time in a penitentiary for pistol-whipping a passenger on a steamboat. The Tigers were commonly referred to derisively as "wharf rats" and a variety of other unsavory names.

Soon another company, the Old Dominion Guards, was recruited by the charismatic and soldierly Major Chatham Roberdeau Wheat, one of the most colorful figures of the day. The thirty-five-year-old Wheat was a native of Virginia but had spent a considerable portion of his life in Louisiana, mostly in New Orleans. Wheat was a lawyer by profession, though he seems to have spent more time as a soldier of fortune than as a practicing attorney. He had fought as a mercenary in Cuba, Mexico, Nicaragua, and Italy. When war broke out at Fort Sumter on April 12, Wheat was one of the most experienced soldiers in either army. At six foot four and 275 pounds and with the social graces of an aristocrat and the fighting spirit of a wild animal, he was a natural leader. Soon a third company, the Walker Guards, was formed. By now, Major Wheat had his mind set on forming a battalion, so he turned command of the Old Dominion Guards over to Captain Obed P. Miller. Later, two more companies were placed under Wheat's command: the Delta Rangers and the Rough and Ready Rangers. The Rough and Readies would later be disbanded and replaced in Wheat's battalion with the Catahoula Guerrillas. In June

into white leggings. On their hats they painted pictures or mottoes such as "Lincoln's Life or a Tiger's Death," and "Tiger by Nature." In addition to the gaudy colors of their uniforms, the men themselves were anything but dull. Mostly young Irishmen, many of them were criminals. In fact, even Captain White had

1861 the 1st Special Battalion was officially commissioned, with Major Wheat as commanding officer. Over the course of the war, a total of 416 men would serve under the battalion's colors. Eventually, Wheat's battalion was permanently assigned to Brigadier General Richard "Dick" Taylor's Louisiana Brigade, along with the 6th, 7th, 8th, and 9th Regiments of Louisiana Volunteers. Major Wheat was finally killed in battle at Gaines's Mill on June 27, 1862. The battalion had been so decimated that it was disbanded in August 1862, and the remaining men were reassigned to regiments serving in Virginia.

While the "tiger" label originally applied only to Wheat's Company B, the Tiger Rifles, the characterization fit the whole battalion. The majority of the men were drinkers, brawlers, thieves, or ex-convicts and were considered the dregs of New Orleans. It wasn't long before all members of Wheat's battalion were called "Tigers." Later, the name "Louisiana Tigers" was applied to all Louisiana infantry, but by that time it was not so much because of their unruly behavior but because of their tremendous courage and ferocity in battle. Louisiana infantry were part of General Robert E. Lee's Army of Northern Virginia and proved to be among the most valuable soldiers. Lee's Tigers, as they came to be known, did their duty and performed with great heroism. They fought from First Manassas to the very last Confederate charge of the war, which they led, near Appomattox Courthouse on April 9, 1865. One gruesome testimony to their courage and fighting spirit was their death rate. By the end of the war it had reached 23 percent. To grasp the enormity of such sacrifice, one must realize that in all wars the number of wounded survivors greatly exceeds the number of dead. Additional testimony to the fighting spirit of the Tigers is revealed in the following farewell address from General Clement Anselm Evans to Colonel Eugene Waggaman's brigade on April 11, 1865:

> The sad hour has arrived when we who served in the Confederate Army so long together must part, at least for a time. . . . But to you, Colonel, and to our brother officers and brother soldiers . . . I claim to say that you can carry with you the proud conscience that in the estimation of your commanders you have done your duty. Tell Louisiana, when you reach her shores, that her sons in the Army of Northern Virginia have made her illustrious upon every battle ground, from first Manassas to the last desperate blow struck by your command on the hills of Appomattox, and tell her, too, that as in the first, so in the last, the enemy fled before the valor of your charging lines. . . . For you, and for your gallant officers and devoted men, I shall always cherish the most pleasing memories, and when I say farewell, it is with a full heart, which beats an earnest prayer to Almighty God for your future happiness.

Major David F. Boyd of the 9th Louisiana Volunteers may have been the first to propose the Tiger nickname the football team would adopt.

premonition of his own impending death. It was Major Boyd who made sure that the last request of his friend and fellow soldier was fulfilled, that he was buried where he fell. Through battle after battle, Major Boyd developed tremendous respect for Wheat's Tigers and for their fearless, and now fallen, commander. The memory of those ferocious Fighting Tigers would stay with Major Boyd long after the din and destruction of war had passed. And in a more peaceful time, the memory of those Tigers and their master would be honored at one of the great universities of the South.

Organized in 1893 by Dr. Charles E. Coates, LSU football also has a colorful history. Dr. Coates obtained membership for LSU in the large Southern Intercollegiate Athletic Association (SIAA), of which LSU was a member until 1923. Dr. Coates, a chemistry professor from Baltimore, served as the head football coach during the team's maiden year. Dr. Coates was so dedicated to establishing football as a sport at LSU that he personally drove nails into shoes to fashion cleats for the team. The team was led by captain and quarterback Ruffin G. Pleasant, who would later serve as state attorney general from 1912 to 1916 and then as governor of Louisiana from 1916 to 1920. The "season" of 1893 consisted of one game, against Tulane University on November 25, which Tulane won 34–0.

One of the soldiers in the 9th Louisiana Volunteers was Major David F. Boyd. His regiment served in Taylor's Louisiana Brigade along with Wheat's 1st Special Battalion, during the Valley campaign of Brigadier General Thomas J. "Stonewall" Jackson. The two junior officers became great friends. Major Boyd was one of the first with whom Wheat shared his

Though off to a slow start, the football program gathered steam rapidly, posting a 2-1-0 record in the 1894 season under head coach Albert P. Simmons, with victories over Natchez (26–0) and Centenary (30–0). The only loss (6–26), and the year's only SIAA game, was against Ole Miss. That year the team captain was a fullback by the colorful name of Samuel Marmaduke Dinwidie Clark.

In 1895, still under Coach Simmons, the team had its first undefeated season, going 3-0-0 under the leadership of captain and quarterback J. E. Snyder. As significant as the accomplishments of the 1895 season were, the team achieved national attention in 1896, with a perfect 6-0-0 record and cochampionship of the SIAA under Coach Allen W. Jeardeau.

The pride and excitement generated by

The 1896 football team that earned the nickname "Tigers." Pictured are, from left: back row (standing), A. E. Chevanne, Wiltz Ledbetter, Justin Daspit, Sidney Snyder, Jim Harp, Lt. Gallop, P. D. Staples, A. T. Barbin, J. T. Westbrook; center row (seated), Hughes Arrighi, Ned Scott, Phil Huych, W. S. Slaughter; front row, George Schoenberger, Sam Gourrier, Sam Atkinson, Gordon Nicholson, A. P. Daspit.

Garland McManus

ATHLETICS

Tiger illustration from the 1911 *Gumbo* yearbook.

Louisiana Tigers came flooding back to professor and former LSU president David F. Boyd and that it is quite likely that it was Boyd who suggested the tiger as the symbol of the university and its football team. While the name was modified slightly in 1955 to "the Fighting Tigers," most still simply refer to the team as "the Tigers."

Naming the team the Tigers seems to have been a logical choice for several reasons. First, the great military tradition of Louisiana's soldiers not only of the Civil War but of all the wars in which they have served is honored and commemorated in the name. Secondly, nothing represents a university like its mascot. The mascot should present a positive and stirring image of the school. Knowing this, many collegiate teams of the past, and even of the present, have borne names of ferocious animals. What more ferocious animal is there than a tiger? To this day, LSU Tiger fans are proud to compare their regal tiger mascot with the dogs, cats, camels, antelopes, sheep, horses, cattle, fish, dolphins, seals, reptiles, amphibians, birds, badgers, armadillos, rodents, kangaroos, apes, bears, pigs, insects, and even banana slug mascots of other college teams. And finally, history has proved the Tiger mascot to be appropriate in yet another way. Like other cats, tigers are most active at night, and one of the many legends surrounding Tiger football is that the team plays

such accomplishments prompted the student body to seek a "nickname" for the team. Time has hidden the story of who first proposed naming the team the Tigers. Some sources credit Coach Coates with the idea. Others suggest that memories of Major Wheat and the better at night. From 1960 to 1990, the team recorded a nighttime winning percentage in Tiger Stadium of 78.5 percent. During the same years, the team won only 39.5 percent of games played during the day. Although the tiger theme caught on instantly, for almost forty years other mascots continued to be suggested. Nicknames brought up for considera-

tion included the Babies, the Roosters, the Alligators, and the Pirates. But with each passing year the tiger theme became more accepted.

From 1896 to 1924, Tiger fans would carry papier-mâché tigers to the football games. Most of these were destroyed by opposing fans almost as quickly as they were made. In time these papier-mâché tigers were given the name

Papier-mâché tigers, like this one created for the 1920 Arkansas football game, were destroyed almost as quickly as they were made.

Clarence A. Ives Jr.

"little eat-'em-ups." This nickname was apparently derived from an incident which occurred during an LSU-Tulane football game. Supposedly one of the LSU players attempted to bite off the ear of a Tulane player.

In 1924, an alumnus donated a small black South American cat, probably similar to a bobcat. He was named "Jerry," and he became LSU's first live mascot. Shortly after arrival his name was changed, as one might guess, to "Little Eat-'em-up." The cat was housed in the operating room of a local veterinarian, Dr. Prescott. Unfortunately, the football team lost all of its conference games that year, so "Little Eat-'em-up" was sent away and the fans went back to using papier-mâché tigers from 1925 to 1936. While the paper tigers were good enough for some, others had a plan to bring a real symbol of the team's spirit to campus.

On January 1, 1936, the LSU Tigers played the TCU Horned Frogs in the Sugar Bowl. This illustration from *Pel-Mell* magazine predates the arrival of the live mascot to the LSU campus by less than a year.

Courtesy Mrs. William Warren Munson

—— THEY WELCOME MIKE ——

◆ On Wednesday, Oct. 24th, the usually quiet campus of the Old War Skule was awakened by one of the most unusual and spontanous demonstration of spirit that has been shown in many years. In the early dawn, like a band of warring natives of the jungle attacking an unsuspecting village, the Students took complete control of the campus, turned out the classes, prevented professors and students with books from entering the campus and pronounced a holiday for President Smith, whether he wanted it or not. The procession then proceeded to the railroad station with the same enthusiasm to give their mascot, Old Mike, a young bengal tiger, as royal a reception as he could ever have received in the jungles of deepest India.

Exactly what this mascot thought concerning the display of spirit will never be known. Throughout the procession he remained calm as he was grand, surveying his new subjects with almost a look of approval.

Reading form left to right:

(1) The band in every day clothes leads the procession.

(2) Gathering around the gym.

(3) They turn out the Law school.

(4) They proceed to the campanile.

(5) Turning out the Music school.

(6) Procession passing the gym.

(7) Early dawn and the crowd gathers.

(8) No Profs—No School !

(9) No more law !

(10) The procession begins.

Pel-Mell issue showing the arrival of the first Bengal tiger to LSU's campus. The date of Mike's arrival is incorrectly listed as October 24.

Courtesy Mrs. William Warren Munson

Mike I (1936–1956)

It was early in the morning on Wednesday, October 21, 1936. The Cadet Corps and student body barred professors from their offices, picketed classrooms, and blocked all entrances to the campus. The band played underneath dormitory windows. According to Russell B. Long, freshmen class president and later United States senator, a few classes began but were quickly closed by students, causing President James M. Smith to declare a holiday and close the university. Just before noon, students paraded through Baton Rouge. Onlookers lined Highland Road, awaiting the entourage arriving from the train station. As the cavalcade approached, students swarmed around to get a look at the new arrival to the LSU family. In the evening they lit a bonfire

Mike I with his keeper, ca. 1936.

and had a grand party. The band played all the versions they knew of "Tiger Rag." Newspapers recorded that Paris may have sung a welcome to General Pershing, New York may have

11

Mike arrives on October 21, 1936. *Gumbo, 1937*

LSU athletic trainer Mike Chambers visits his namesake in his first home at the Baton Rouge City Park Zoo. *Pop Strange*

showered Charles Lindberg with ticker tape, but LSU students staged a campus strike equal to none to welcome their new tiger mascot to campus.

Freshmen with strike signs picketed all entrances to campus on the day Mike arrived. *Gumbo, 1937*

Two years earlier, in 1934, a decision had been made that would forever change life on the LSU campus. Athletic Department trainer Chellis "Mike" Chambers, Athletic Director T. P. Heard, swimming pool manager and intramural swimming coach William G. "Hickey" Higginbotham, and LSU law student Ed Laborde decided to bring a real tiger to LSU, then known as the "Ole War Skule." They raised $750, collecting twenty-five cents from each student, and purchased a two-hundred-pound, one-year-old tiger from the Little Rock Zoo. They found him with the help of LSU student Ken Kavanaugh (later to become an All-American end), who had heard about a tiger being available from Little Rock and had notified Chambers. It seems that a circus tiger named Sheik had been banished to the Little Rock Zoo in 1928 after attacking a trainer. At the zoo Sheik was paired with a female tiger named Sue. Their cub was born on Thursday, October 10, 1935, and, like his father, was originally named Sheik. But his name was changed to Mike in honor of Chambers, the man most responsible for bringing him to LSU. Student body president Glen Olds had put the tiger name change to a vote of the student body, and it was overwhelmingly approved. Interestingly, Mike I must have remembered his original name because even years later Hickey Higginbotham could get him to roar just by calling "Sheik."

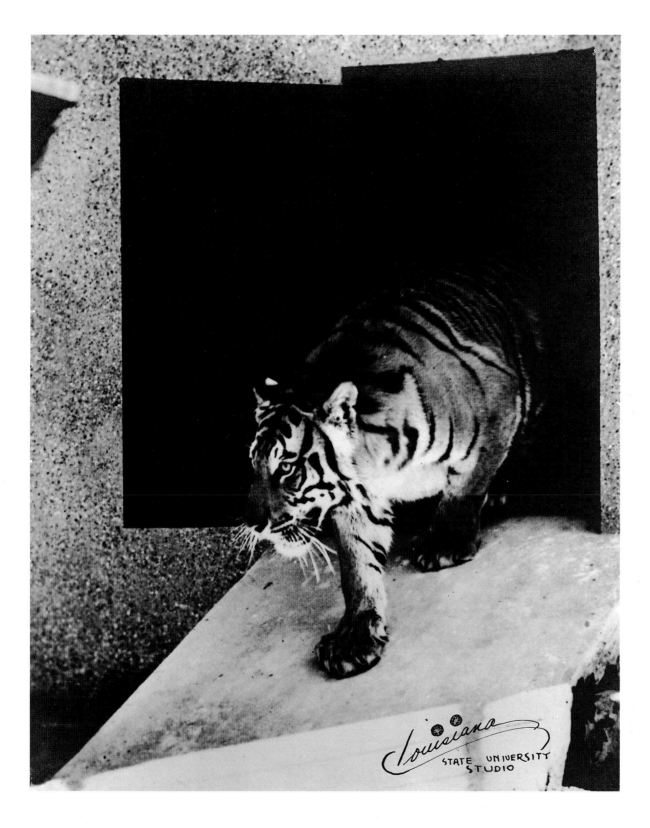

A portrait of Mike by the
LSU Studio.

Mike gets a new home near the football stadium.

Elevation plan courtesy Somdal Associates

WEST · ELEVATION

Mike I assumed his responsibilities just three days after arriving on campus. On October 24, 1936, Mike traveled to Shreveport to help LSU defeat Arkansas 19–7 under the leadership of team captain Bill May and Coach Bernie H. Moore. There was a rousing halftime show in Mike's honor and an increased excitement for LSU football that was noticeable to all. Mr. Gordon E. Doré, former member of the LSU Board of Supervisors, attended that first game. He said, "It was fantastic! It was during the depression days. Everyone needed

Mike's new home, completed in 1937.

anything that they could get to sort of pump them up a little bit. . . . The fact that our university was going to have a live tiger was absolutely fantastic! It was good for the university and good for the state. . . . It happened for the university and the state at a very special time." Throughout the day LSU fans chanted, "Let's feed the tiger a Razorback"! After such a wonderful initiation to LSU football, Mike began to travel with the team regularly.

When he wasn't traveling, Mike I stayed at the City Park Zoo under the care of the keeper, a Mr. Barry. The "zoo" was a small facility just north of the LSU campus, overlooking the LSU lakes. Mike quickly established a habit of rising at about 4:00 A.M. to roar a greeting to the new day. As a youngster, Mike I was a gentle tiger, regularly enjoying a lot of physical contact. That would change over time, as Mike reached adulthood. Although life was good at the zoo, Mike was moved down the hill onto the LSU campus after he got his leg and paw between the bars of his cage and slashed Higginbotham. A tiger house and a 27- by 34-foot outdoor cage were built next to the football stadium in 1937, at a cost of about $3,500. Mike's new home was dedicated by Governor Richard W. Leche prior to an LSU-Alabama baseball game on April 13 of that year. Records indicate that at the time, it cost about $600 per year to feed the tiger.

Governor Leche was a great fan of the new tiger. Richard W. Leche Jr. recalls a humorous conversation that took place in 1936 before an LSU football game, between the Governor and Porter "Eddie" Bryant. Bryant was a local vegetable vendor and LSU fan who claimed that his vegetables were "educated" because they were grown near the university. He therefore called himself the "Educated Vegetable Man." Shortly after Mike's arrival on campus, Bryant had named himself Mike's manager and regularly accompanied the tiger. While viewing Mike on the football field, the governor turned to Bryant and asked, "What will you do if he gets out of his cage?" Byrant quickly responded, "I'd get in it!"

From the beginning, Mike I was the re-

Mike speaks his mind in October of 1938.

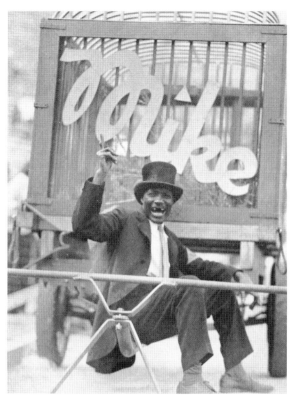

Porter "Eddie" Bryant, known as "The Educated Vegetable Man," declared himself Mike's Head Keeper the day of Mike's arrival on campus.

Gumbo, *1937*

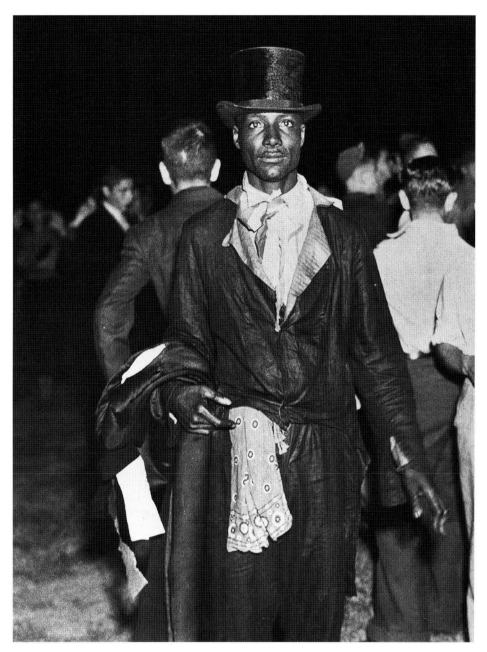

Porter Bryant, Mike's self-appointed manager.

sponsibility of the Athletic Department. For many years, Hickey Higginbotham had general oversight of Mike. Mike's day-to-day care was provided by students hired by the Athletic Department. In addition to a monthly salary, initially twenty-five dollars, students received a parking pass that allowed them to park by the Animal Science building where Mike's food was stored. They could also park near his cage. Even then, choice parking spots were highly coveted. Another bonus was getting to use a Ford convertible for the weekend. Of course the car was to be used to pull Mike's trailer before the football games, but the students couldn't see any harm in putting a few miles on it over the weekend before returning it to the dealership.

Mike I plays with his handler, W. G. Higginbotham, ca. 1937.

Leon Trice, Baton Rouge Advocate

Mike's first student caretakers were members of the swimming and diving team. From the 1940s to the mid-1950s, the student caretaker position was passed down within the Sigma Chi fraternity and later through Theta Xi. Zeta Beta Tau fraternity, which is no longer active on the LSU campus, cared for Mike II

and Mike III from 1957 until 1968. During much of the 1970s, two members of Kappa Sigma cared for Mike III and Mike IV. The lives of the many tiger "keepers" are themselves interesting stories. Many of them have gone on to become successful professionals and businessmen. Charles Fourrier, Mike's keeper from 1939 to 1942, served in World War II and lost his life in an aircraft landing accident at Pearl Harbor. Osce R. Jones, a tiger keeper who became a P-51 fighter pilot, was shot down over France and spent time in a German POW camp.

Mike I attended football games as far away as Birmingham to help inspire the team to victory. Often he traveled by train, but usually he traveled in his $300 trailer, donated by the Louisiana Highway Department. During Mike's first few years as mascot, he traveled around the state in the summer as a publicity agent for the football team. He also accompanied the swim team occasionally as they traveled around Louisiana giving swimming and

Governor Richard W. Leche (foreground) on the field with Mike I, ca. 1936. To his left is Lt. Gov. Earl K. Long.

Richard W. Leche Papers, MSS 2060, LLMV Collections, LSU Libraries, Baton Rouge

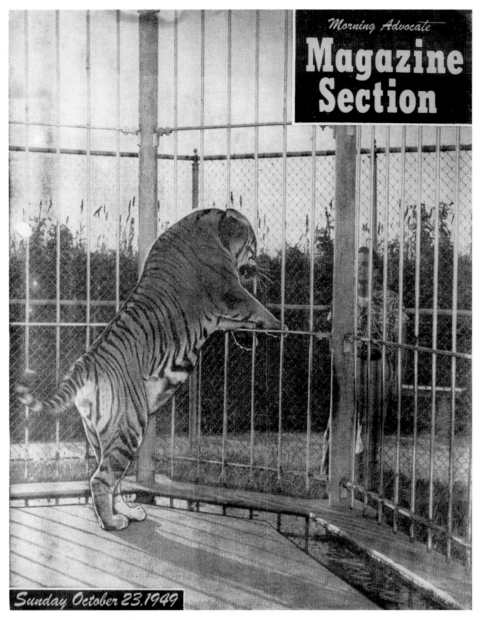

Morning Advocate

Magazine Section

Sunday October 23,1949

The Sunday *Morning Advocate* Magazine Section cover featured Mike in his favorite pose in 1949.

diving exhibitions and helping to dedicate new swimming pool facilities. In 1949, relates former LSU swimmer Fred Frey Jr., when Hickey Higginbotham and members of the LSU swim team were returning from an event near Lake Charles they stopped at a gas station in the town of Kinder. Of course the live tiger immediately drew a crowd. Higginbotham joked to the gathering onlookers that it was "time to let Mike out for a walk." The local sheriff, who was in the crowd, reached for his gun and said, "If you let that tiger out, y'all are going to jail!"

Mike I was unusual for a tiger in that he liked to stand up in his trailer while traveling. This was sometimes a problem, since he could spray urine right into the seats of the car towing him. That happened on at least two separate occasions during parades down Third Street in Baton Rouge. In both cases, a group of coed cheerleaders were sitting up on the back seat of the towing car, a convertible, when all of a sudden they started screaming and diving for cover. Both Hickey Higginbotham and Jere D. Melilli would later laugh about it, but at the time they didn't dare!

During his tenure, Mike I eventually traveled to all of the schools in the Southeastern Conference. Occasionally, Mike and Higginbotham would get back into Baton Rouge after midnight. Rather than going to the trouble of returning Mike to his enclosure at such an hour, Higginbotham would park Mike's trailer inside his garage at home. The neighbors got used to hearing the sounds of a tiger coming from the Higginbotham garage!

It seems that once Mike I even got a nighttime tour of parts of Baton Rouge, courtesy of his student caretakers. According to Gordon

20

Homecoming trophies adorn the top of Mike's trailer in 1942.

Courtesy Mrs. Osce R. Jones

Doré, Mike's keepers loaded him up and took him into town one night, making sure that people saw the tiger in his trailer. Then they returned to campus and quickly unloaded him. When they returned to the same parts of town with the trailer empty and the gate swinging open, they got an entirely different response. People were convinced that the tiger was loose in their neighborhood, and many went scurrying for the safety of their homes. The students encouraged the deception by asking people if they'd seen the tiger. The story goes that parts of the city closed up early that night!

Mike I ate a hearty daily meal of eight to twelve pounds of meat, sometimes covered with cod-liver oil, a slab of salt, and often, as a special treat, three eggs and a quart of milk to maintain his sleek coat. Several have said that Mike I would refuse to eat if he were being watched. Of course during World War II Mike's allotment of meat was rationed like everyone else's. He did not like this one bit. Former students living in the stadium dormitories at the time have told of Mike keeping them awake at night with his roaring. Anyone who has heard a tiger roar can imagine how difficult it would be to go to sleep with that

A view of the tiger's cage taken from North Stadium dormitory, ca. 1945. During the war, Mike kept many a stadium dorm student awake with his protests for more food.

Courtesy Frank M. O'Quinn

terrifying sound. There was even a plan to transport Mike to the Audubon Zoo for the duration of the war so that he would have access to adequate food. LSU students were not very excited about seeing their beloved mascot housed in Tulane territory. Some students even forced student body president Hugh O'Connor and vice president Jeff Burkett to ride around campus on parade in Mike's trailer, pulled by seven male students, prior to a meeting with university officials to discuss the transfer. Finally, with so much opposition from the student body the plans to ship Mike to New Orleans were scrapped.

When fully grown, Mike I was of average size at 450 pounds. Mike definitely had some dislikes. Although he enjoyed cooling off in his water trough, several caretakers recall that he became very agitated when sprayed with a hose. Neither was Mike I overly fond of people, as several of his caretakers would later attest. Eddy Contine, one of Mike's early student caretakers, once found himself face-to-face with the tiger. Contine had forgotten to close a gate before entering his enclosure. He was so frightened, all he could stutter was: "Hic . . . Hic . . . Hickey!" Hickey Higginbotham grabbed a pan and started running it along the cage, calling out, "Sheik!" That distracted Mike long enough for the terrified stu-

Mike enjoys a hearty meal in 1941.

Courtesy Mrs. Osce R. Jones

Students in 1946 hold up the traditional "Rag" claimed each year by the winner of the LSU-Tulane football game, an annual rivalry at that time.

Courtesy University Relations

dent to make his escape. Similar near catastrophes occurred when Mike's next caretakers, Charles Fourrier and Osce R. Jones, on separate occasions, mistakenly forgot to close the gate separating themselves from Mike. Fortunately for all, they managed to escape from the cage before Mike decided to attack. A few years later, Brittain Briggs once got too close to the cage while chipping ice off the lock. Seeing the opportunity, Mike reached a paw through the bars and slapped Briggs to the ground with one swat. Later, former LSU student Bob Bogan recalls accompanying Mike to Austin for a game against the University of Texas. Bogan made the mistake of putting his finger into Mike's cage. Mike promptly bit it, sending Bogan on a trip to the local hospital. The attending physician wouldn't believe his story until it was confirmed by another physician who happened to be an LSU graduate and assured him that, yes, LSU did own a tiger. Bogan wasn't the first to have such a close call

Cheerleaders in 1950 pump up the fans from atop Mike's cage.

slashed Melilli's shoe. There is no doubt that Mike was trying to get the student's foot inside the cage. Confirming that Mike I did not care much for his keepers, Melilli recalls how Mike knew the sound of the squeaky door on his car, a 1941 Studebaker. Jere could squeak that door from a hundred yards away, and that was enough to get the tiger fighting mad.

Mike I doesn't seem to have been too fond of other animals either. At least he kept up the age-old conflict between cats and dogs, and this time the cats won. Jere Melilli recalls a time when he had just opened the door into Mike's house, and out of nowhere a very small dog ran past him and right up to Mike. Melilli watched in horror as Mike reached through the bars and pulled the dog in with him in one fell swoop. Melilli says that in a matter of seconds all that was left of the dog was his collar and a few tufts of hair. Mike had made a snack of him! That and the shoe-slashing incident served as permanent reminders to Melilli of just how fast, powerful, and dangerous these animals are.

Mike I had almost as eventful a life as Mike IV would have forty years later. At least twice, in 1941 and 1953, students threw birthday parties for Mike. In 1941 a musical revue, "Hold That Tiger" was scheduled to coincide with a rally for the LSU–Texas A&M game. Of course Mike was the guest of honor. During the show about 150 Aggies tried to break up

with Mike. Jere Melilli's brush with Mike was even closer. He recalls a time when he was inside Mike's house trying to coax him out, when his foot slipped toward Mike. In an instant, Mike reached through the bars and

Contemplative Mike.

the party but were thwarted by LSU cadets. Then, in 1953, the student body declared the weekend of Saturday, October 10, "Mike's Birthday Party." The theme of the party was, "Knock out Kentucky for the love of Mike." A large birthday cake, complete with peppermint goalposts and over a thousand candle "spectators," was made and generously donated by Mr. Jack Sabin, owner of The Goal Post, a local restaurant. Of course in a bottom layer of the cake was a raw roast for Mike. The celebration was campuswide and included the football coaches and team, the Tiger band, the Purple Jackets, the Pershing Rifles, the Cadet Corps, and several dormitory groups. In spite of all the hoopla, the game ended in a 6–6 tie.

In 1944 alumnus and former LSU track star Lieutenant Alfred M. L. "Smokey" Sanders honored Mike by having his name and picture painted on the nose of his B-24 bomber. Underneath Mike's name and image was also painted *Spirit of LSU,* the name Sanders gave

This poster of the *Spirit of LSU* was painted in the 1970s using Mike III's image. The original plane was painted in Sudbury, England, by someone who had never seen the real Mike.

Painting by Glenn Gore

The only known photograph of the *Spirit of LSU.*

the plane. The bomber was proudly flown in many combat missions over Europe during World War II and was the only aircraft of WWII named after Louisiana State University. Mission records reveal that the Spirit of LSU was often the formation leader. On May 28, 1944, just nine days before D day, Sanders was to take the *Spirit* on another mission, but because the bomber was known as one of the fastest in the squadron, another officer pulled rank and took the aircraft instead. Sanders was

The crew of the *Spirit of LSU* (Lieutenant Sanders standing far left).

assigned a slower bomber for the day's mission. On that day, Sanders and his crew were hit by flak while on a bombing run over Germany. In spite of heavy damage to his ship, Sanders managed to release his bombs and turned back toward England. Not able to make it across the channel, all the crew members bailed out, and the aircraft crashed in Belgium. Sanders was captured, but he escaped with help from Belgian nationals. He returned to England on September 9, 1944. Sanders' love for LSU was shared by his young bride Mildred ("Millie"), also an LSU graduate. Millie learned of her husband's capture just days after their son was born. Not knowing whether she would see her tiger again, she named their son "Mike."

As Mike I passed middle age, many were concerned that time was growing short for him to sire a cub. After all, he would eventually need an heir. Two attempts were made to send him on a quest for love at the Audubon Zoo. However, in each case the LSU student body blocked the efforts. They did not relish the idea of their beloved mascot going to New Orleans. The Crescent City was considered hostile territory, home to arch rival Tulane. Finally, in July 1945, the student body agreed by a vote of 403 to 4 that Mike should travel to the R. M. Taylor Zoo in Jackson, Mississippi.

Lieutenant Alfred M. L. "Smokey" Sanders had a picture of Mike painted on the nose of his B-24 bomber, dubbed the *Spirit of LSU*.

"The cage was empty Friday" was the caption that ran with this photograph reporting that Mike had died.

© *1956 New Orleans* Times-Picayune

Awaiting him there was a lovely three-and-a-half-year-old female tiger named Desdemona.

E. L. Upp, an LSU cheerleader and Mike's student caretaker at the time, went along on the trip to Mississippi. Quite a stir was caused everywhere they stopped along the way. At one gas station in Mississippi, Mike sprayed a little boy all dressed up in his Sunday best who had come out to see him. The shocked boy ran off to tell his mother. One can imagine her disbelief when he told her he was sprayed by a tiger! Once unloaded from his trailer at the zoo, Mike immediately began to get nervous, perhaps because of the strange environment or because he sensed the female nearby. Eventually the two tigers, separated by some fencing, sighted one another. Desdemona saw Mike first and gave out a snort and a growl. But instead of returning the greeting, Mike jumped back in such fear that he landed flat on his back. LSU staff were concerned that the Ole Miss faithful would find out about the incident and use it mockingly to their advantage. Fortunately, word didn't get out that Mike was afraid of a female tiger. Though Mike stayed at the Jackson zoo for a few months, he and Desdemona never really hit it off, and he eventually returned without having had the opportunity to breed. It was feared that the risk of injury to one or both of the tigers was too great to allow contact.

When LSU traveled to the Jan 1, 1947, Cotton Bowl, Hickey Higginbotham hitched Mike's cage to his car and headed for Dallas. When they left Baton Rouge it was 85 degrees and sunny. When they reached Shreveport it was 15 degrees and sleeting. Not wanting to expose Mike to more inclement weather, Higginbotham got permission from Alfred Glassell to shelter Mike in his warehouse for a few days. Unfortunately, the night watchman wasn't told of Mike's arrival. When the poor man entered the warehouse on his nightly rounds and shined his flashlight on Mike, the tiger let out a growl that nearly scared the man to death. It is rumored that the man never completely recovered from the experience.

On December 1, 1950, one of the most famous episodes in the history of the tiger mascots occurred. The most reliable account of the incident comes from Tom Freeman, who frequently assisted Mike's caretaker David Melilli. It came about when Mike I was taken to New Orleans for a game against Tulane. It was customary when traveling to New Orleans for a football game for Mike to avoid the Saturday traffic by arriving a day early. Mike would frequently stay at Ye Olde College Inn, under the eye of a night watchman. On this occasion, the watchman went to the rear of the inn to find a tarpaulin to cover the trailer. Melilli, who had gone to the Roosevelt Hotel, returned to the inn about ten minutes later, only to find Mike missing! He then woke Freeman, and the two of them drove around New Orleans listening for a tiger's roar. What they didn't know was that Mike had been hidden in the Tulane football stadium and was being guarded by Tulane students and local police. The plan hatched by the Tulane students was for their cheerleaders to return Mike to the LSU cheerleaders at halftime. When Melilli and Freeman found Mike, they attempted to retrieve their precious mascot, but the police would not give him up. Finally, at literally the last hour, LSU athletic director T. P. "Red" Heard demanded Mike's return. He was reluctantly handed over. The LSU students had just enough time to remove the blue and green crepe streamers from the trailer as Mike was entering the stadium. Unfortunately, there was no time to remove the green paint from the trailer, where the Tulane tigernappers had proudly announced the name of the offending university. This incident served to fuel the rivalry between the schools for many years.

In his many travels, Mike I miraculously survived at least two automobile accidents. The most serious occurred on November 25, 1951, on U.S. Highway 71, about fifteen miles north of Coushatta, Louisiana. Mike was returning in triumph from a 45–7 victory over Villanova in Shreveport. A motorist drove onto the highway shoulder and attempted to pass Mike's trailer. Caretaker David Melilli, who was towing Mike's trailer at the time, was himself trying to pass a slower vehicle. Melilli swerved back into his lane, but in the process Mike's trailer flipped over into a ditch. Fortunately, nobody, including Mike, was injured. A wrecker from Coushatta was called out and righted the trailer. After clearance from state trooper E. C. Clinton, the entourage was on its way again.

In 1953, Mike I was ceremonially honored with a varsity letter from Kenner Day, then national president of the L Club. Also in 1953, university officials decided that, due to advancing age, Mike's traveling days were over. Unfortunately, that policy appears not to have been followed completely. On November 27, 1954, Mike was once again on his way to New Orleans for the LSU-Tulane game. A sudden stop by his caretaker, Bob Dodwell, caused Mike's trailer to jackknife and turn over on Airline Highway. Although Dodwell was slightly injured, Mike was once again unharmed.

In 1955, the aged Mike I became ill. Dr. Joe Dixon of the LSU Department of Veterinary Science was asked by golf coach Harry Taylor to provide veterinary care for the tiger. There-

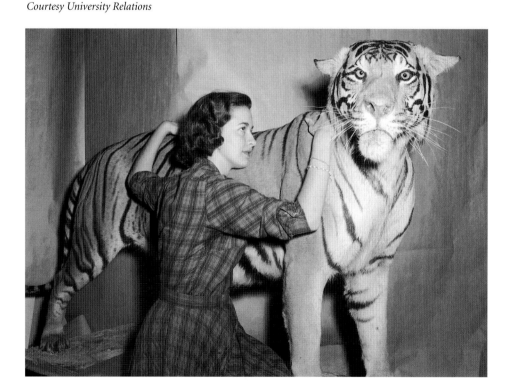

Mike I and coed Betty Ann Landry.

Courtesy University Relations

30

after, while the Athletic Department retained authority over the tiger's day-to-day life, Mike I and subsequent tigers would have a veterinarian to attend to their medical needs. This was a significant advance in the overall care of the LSU tiger mascots.

Mike I died on Friday, June 29, 1956, of complications associated with kidney disease. In backyards all over Louisiana, children held mock funerals in his honor. Others hung his photograph, draped in black crepe paper. Many people who had been present on campus at his arrival or had grown up visiting him mourned his passing. He was twenty years and eight months old at his death and had reigned at LSU for nearly twenty years. Without a doubt Mike I created a legacy in which Mike the Tiger has come to symbolize the heart and soul of LSU athletics.

Mike I began a long tradition as a proud symbol of LSU, and he was featured in numerous publications, including Paul D. Buchanan's *Famous Animals of the States.* Following Mike's death, a fund was established to perpetuate his memory by mounting his pelt in a lifelike manner and displaying him at the university's Louisiana Museum of Natural History. Museum taxidermist P. A. Daigre oversaw the painstaking process. Mike I remains proudly displayed in the museum to this day, the patriarch of a long and great LSU tradition.

After his death, the University's Louisiana Museum of Natural History's taxidermist P. A. Daigre oversaw the painstaking process of mounting Mike's pelt in a lifelike pose.

Courtesy University Relations

MIKE I'S STUDENT CARETAKERS

1936–37: L. C. Aycock

1937–38: Preston Vallas

1938–39: Elliot "Eddy" Contine

1939–42: Charles Fourrier

1942–43: Osce R. Jones

1943–44: Charles Upp

1944–45: George Thompson

1945–46: E. Loy Upp

1946–47: H. Staton Barlow

1947–49: Brittain Briggs

1949–51: David Melilli

1951–53: Jere D. Melilli

1953–55: Bob Dodwell

1955–56: Gene Smith

Mike II was six months old
when this picture was taken
by Bob Morgan.

Mike II (1956–1958)

On July 1, 1956, just a few days after the death of the beloved Mike I, Representative Kenneth Deshotel of St. Landry introduced a resolution in the Louisiana legislature endorsing the purchase of another tiger. The resolution also conveyed sympathy to the LSU community for the loss of Mike I. Deshotel stated that he hoped that the new tiger would be called "Mike II." On campus, the Mike the Tiger Fund was launched by student body president Enos Parker and fellow students Vic Koepp and John Nunn to purchase "Mike Junior." Students away from campus for the summer were encouraged to mail in their contributions. It was hoped that a new tiger could be found by the start of the next football season. The first game was scheduled for September

33

The first Mike II was chosen over his littermate because of his larger paws.

new tiger would come equally from student fees and the Athletic Department. This was an important step toward assuring proper care of Mike II as well as his successors.

To this day the story of Mike II remains shrouded in mystery. Mike II was born on February 28, 1956, at the Audubon Zoo in New Orleans. He was the son of a four-year-old male named Jim, originally from the Cincinnati Zoo. His mother was a lovely five-year-old tiger named Carol, who had some circus experience. Mike II was one of two tiger cubs being considered for sale to LSU by the Audubon Zoo. He was selected because his paws were larger than those of the other cub. Mike II arrived secretly on the LSU campus on September 28, 1956. The young tiger was held overnight in the football stadium, guarded in two-hour shifts by members of the student council against any would-be Tulane pranksters. The tiger sitters included Don Lartigue, Fred Hartdegan, Ed Thornhill, Laurie Sledge, John Nunn, and Tom Young. Mike's unveiling occurred the next day, September 29, opening day of the new football season. An academic holiday was declared, and the celebrations began. A parade led by the LSU band wound through downtown Baton Rouge. Parade participants decorated their cars with streamers and signs bearing slogans such as "I Like Mike" and "Dig That Crazy Cat." Later, there was a general campus open house, a drill

29 against the Aggies of Texas A&M. There wasn't much time, but the money was quickly raised. On August 4, the LSU Board of Supervisors passed a resolution stating that caretaker salaries and maintenance costs for the

Local banking institutions issued tiger banks like the one above to customers upon the birth of children in their family during the late 1950s.

This tiger child's bank is from a Shreveport bank.

A parade led by the LSU band was held in downtown Baton Rouge to celebrate the arrival of the new Mike.

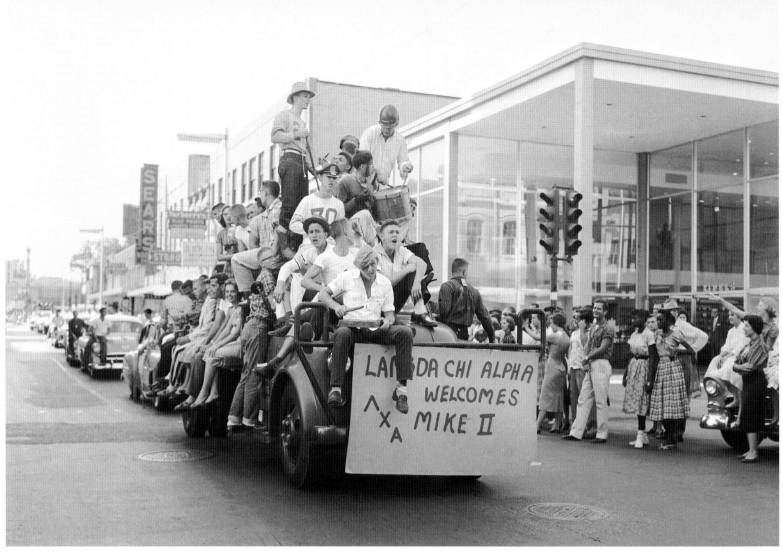

The Lamda Chi Alpha float in Mike's parade.

Courtesy University Relations

routine, a salute by the Pershing Rifles, and a welcoming ceremony honoring the new, regal addition to the LSU family. During the ceremony, a check for $1,500 was presented to George Douglas, superintendent of the Audubon Zoo, by Enos Parker. Several persons who had played prominent roles in the life of Mike I returned to campus to honor his heir. Among them were two former cheerleaders, sisters Juliette and Marie Louise Bonnette; former athletic trainer Mike Chambers; 1936 stu-

dent body president Glen Olds; and former traveling companion of Mike I, Ed Laborde. In the evening there were parties in Mike's honor.

Legend has it that less than a month after his arrival at LSU, Mike II died of pneumonia at only eight months of age during a six-game losing streak. Reportedly, Mike II was then secretly buried under a willow tree along the Mississippi River by newly appointed athletic director Jim Corbett, campus police chief C. R. "Dick" Anderson, and LSU Athletic Depart-

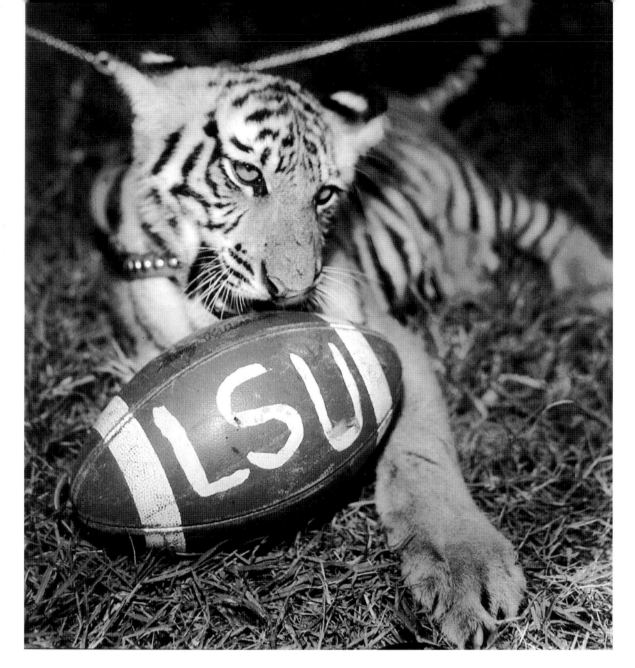

A young Mike II chews on a football. A color version of this image first appeared on the cover of *Dixie Roto* magazine on October 21, 1956.

Philip Guarisco, © 1956 New Orleans Times-Picayune

ment business manager Jack Gilmore. According to Gilmore, a campus police officer found the tiger dead at 1:00 A.M. that October morning. Jim Corbett was immediately called in. Inside the tiger cage, reflecting on the gravity of the situation, Corbett said to others on the scene, "I can see the newspaper stories now.

The football team is so bad that even the tiger couldn't bear the shame." To explain Mike's absence, a statement was issued in the LSU *Daily Reveille* on October 23 saying that Mike was having trouble adjusting to his enclosure and was therefore being kept inside "until he becomes more accustomed to the excitement

The second Mike II.

Courtesy Chico Moore

of being a mascot." Jim Corbett Jr., eleven years old at the time, says that his father never told him what happened next, but he recalls phone calls being made in a frantic effort to find another tiger. It was Jack Gilmore who lo-cated a cub of the right age at the Woodland Park Zoo in Seattle. Gilmore says that he arranged for the cub to be delivered to the Audubon Zoo in New Orleans.

In addition to Gilmore's testimony, several

The second Mike II resting in his trailer.
Erby M. Aucoin Jr.

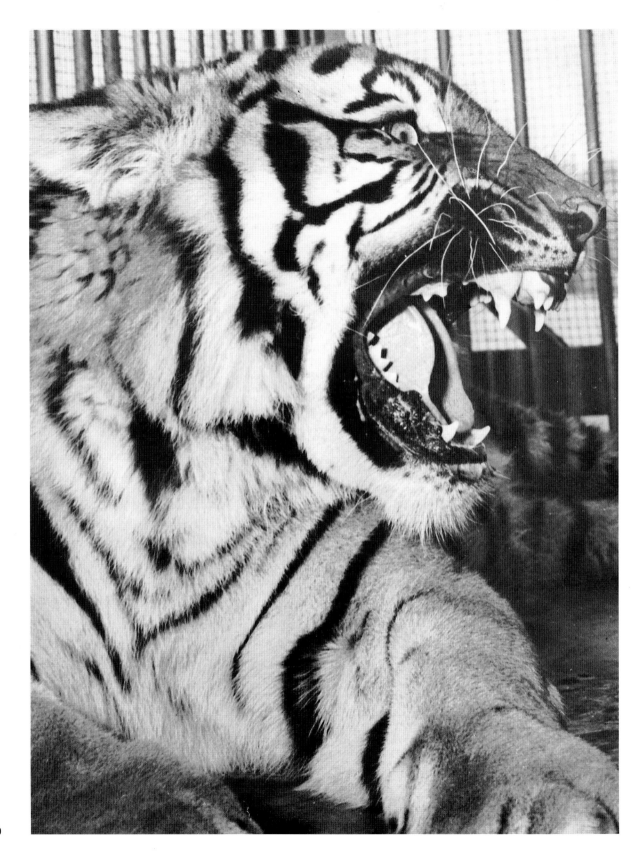

Mike II looks as if he could
be heard all over campus
when this photo was taken.

Gumbo, *1958*

Cheerleaders on the brand new "tiger chariot," custom-built for Mike, ca. 1957.

Cheerleaders from the 1956 football season ride the top of the original trailer.

Gumbo, *1957*

pieces of evidence support the legend that the original Mike II died and was replaced by another young tiger. However, few of these facts were widely known at the time. Records from the Woodland Park Zoo in Seattle do list a litter of three cubs born February 24, 1956, almost the same date as the tiger born at Audubon Zoo. There is no record of what became of those cubs. It is certainly possible that one of those cubs was brought to LSU from Seattle via New Orleans and given the name Mike II. Records from the Audubon Zoo for

Tulane Green Wave graffiti on Mike's home from the 1956 football season is painted over, under the watchful of eyes of several disgruntled LSU students.
Gumbo, *1957*

1956 refer to a tiger cub being purchased from the Seattle zoo and transferred to Baton Rouge. Photographs of Mike II taken before and after his convalescence are clearly of two different tigers. Careful examination reveals that while very similar, the facial markings of the two tigers, unique as human fingerprints, are indeed different. When Mike II was once again allowed to leave his tiger house that November, he seemed to have grown at a tremendous rate. Various records from the time list Mike's weight at 65 pounds in September 1956 and 130 pounds by November 28. There is

Mike II shows his teeth with a growl, ca. 1956.

A wreath is hung by SGA vice president Mippy Jackson to mourn the death of the second tiger on the LSU campus.

Courtesy University Relations

even record of a necropsy (an autopsy of an animal) being performed on a tiger cub at a medical center in New Orleans during the time that Mike was supposedly being kept in isolation. Nevertheless, all rumors of the death and replacement of Mike II were denied. The official story was that Mike II had finally adjusted to life as a mascot, that he was in great health, and that the necropsied cub was actually one of Mike's litter mates.

The second Mike II (if indeed there was a "phoney feline") reigned at LSU for only one season. He died at the Audubon Zoo on May 15, 1958, of complications associated with multiple fractures to his left rear leg. It was not known exactly how or when the leg was injured. There was speculation that the injury occurred when he jumped from a pedestal in his cage to the concrete floor below, and the injury is known to have occurred sometime near the end of the previous September. Mike was taken to the Audubon Zoo in April for treatment of the leg, but an uncontrollable infection arose.

Mike was taken to Charity Hospital in New Orleans for a necropsy. Maxine Marionneaux, a medical technology student at the hospital, tells of finding Mike II on a table in the morgue. Maxine, who worked in the emergency room laboratory next door, had gone to the morgue in the middle of the night to use the phone. Marionneaux recalls, "When I walked into the morgue, there was that huge tiger laid out on that table. At the time, it wasn't funny. I couldn't believe it." She'd been exposed to some unusual things in the morgue but never a tiger!

Despite his death at a young age, at least one very positive development came during Mike II's short reign. In September, 1957, a brand new, custom-built "tiger chariot" was purchased. It was built by Sam Miley of Miley Horse Trailers in Ft. Worth, Texas. This "tiger taxi" replaced the much smaller and less stable cage that had been used to transport Mike I and Mike II. The new trailer would serve as the traveling cage for Mike II and his successors until 1997, when it was replaced after forty years of service. The design of the trailer was so good that few modifications were made in the construction of the 1997 model.

MIKE II'S STUDENT CARETAKERS

1956–57: Gene Smith

1957–58: Sidney S. Miller

1958: Bill Levenson

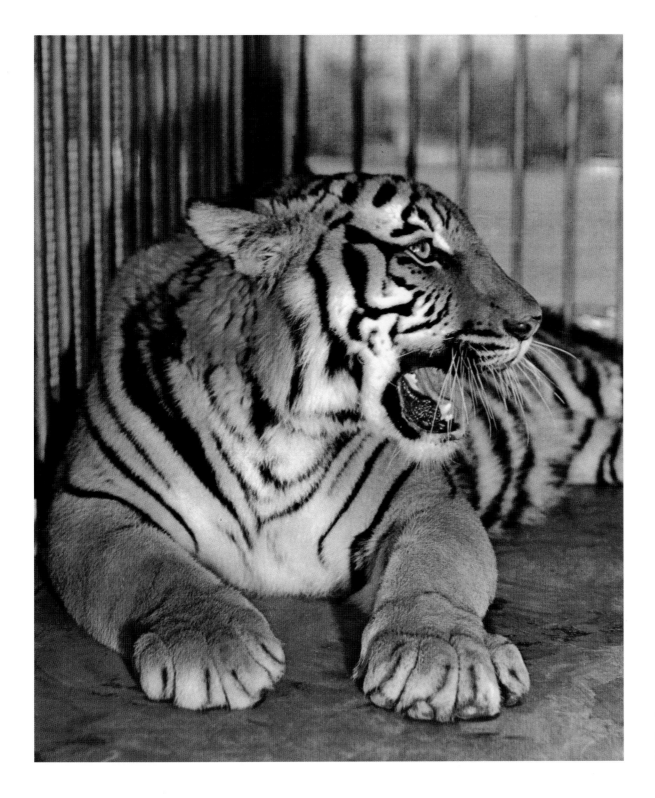

The second Mike II appeared
on this color poster, ca. 1957.

Erby M. Aucoin Jr.

Mike III in 1968.

Mike III (1958–1976)

Just in time for the national championship football season of 1958, Jim Corbett and Jack Gilmore located and purchased Mike III, coincidentally, from the Seattle zoo. This new mascot was born on Tuesday, November 26, 1957, and arrived at LSU in late August 1958. The LSU student body raised $1,500 for his purchase and transportation (though the final purchase price was only $950, with an additional $100 for transportation). Mike III was flown to Chicago on "Flying Tiger Airlines," then on to New Orleans on Delta Airlines. A five-cent "tradition fee" was assessed each student for the tiger's care. Mike III was introduced to the general public at the first home game of the 1958 season, on October 4 against Hardin-Simmons University. LSU won 20–6.

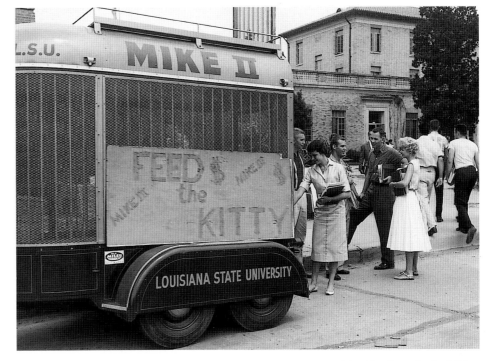

Raising funds again for Mike.
Baton Rouge Advocate

Mike III in the fall of 1959. The photographer bravely entered Mike's outer cage and was fine until the caretaker got Mike to roar *(left)*. When the flash went off, Mike stared straight at the photographer and roared even louder. The photographer was terrified, but the shot was worth it: the official tiger logo still in use today was copied from the resulting photo *(right)*.

Erby M. Aucoin Jr.

According to Mike III's first student caretaker, Bill Levenson, the new mascot adjusted easily to life at LSU. Mike III lived a long and healthy life on about twelve pounds of horsemeat per day along with cod-liver oil, vitamins, and minerals. Mike was also regularly given freshly killed chickens, which Dr. Dixon had heard were good for tigers. Though Mike III's long life was relatively uneventful, it was not completely without incident. He broke both rear legs shortly after arrival at LSU, probably while jumping onto the hard cage floor. Fortunately, he was laid up for only six weeks, and the limbs healed quickly under Dr.

Dixon's care. Douglas Davidson, Mike's caretaker from 1959 to 1961, and his friend and assistant Howard Dumont report that before one LSU-Tulane football game, some Tulane students threw green paint all over Mike. Dr. Dixon, with the help of several student assistants, anesthetized Mike and examined him to determine whether he had ingested any of the paint. Fortunately, it appeared that he had not. After that incident the caretakers would lock Mike up for up to a week before the LSU-Tulane football game to protect him from pranksters. Otherwise, student caretakers from the era report that Mike III was rarely ill and required very little veterinary care. He did need a root canal procedure at one time, but he appeared to have weathered that well. Also, according to Joel Samuels, Mike's caretaker from 1965 to 1968, the surface of his outer enclosure had been coated with a purple and gold rubberized material that prevented his claws from wearing normally. As a result, Mike's claws would overgrow and had to be trimmed by Dr. Dixon every six months. After

Dr. William Oglesby (*left,* then head of the Veterinary Science Department), Dr. Joe Dixon *(center),* and Dr. Robert Lank put casts on Mike's broken legs.

Baton Rouge Advocate

one particularly bothersome overgrown nail was removed, the new floor was too. Mike III was a very hearty tiger. On at least one occasion temperatures dropped to fourteen degrees inside his tiger house, freezing his water. Although he seemed to tolerate it well, a kerosene heater was quickly added to warm things up a bit, and fresh water was brought in regularly until the cold snap ended.

It was apparent to his keepers early on that Mike III was a much calmer tiger than Mike II (either of them!) had been. His calm nature may have saved the lives of at least four of his keepers. The first was Alvin Meyer Jr., Mike's student caretaker from 1961 to 1963. One day he forgot to make sure that Mike was safely locked in his tiger house before he went in to clean the enclosure. Going about his business, Meyer came face-to-face with the big cat. Mike had wandered out of his house looking for his twelve pounds of horsemeat. Fortunately for all, he was more interested in his supper than he was in the student. Needless to say, Meyer beat a hasty retreat to allow Mike to dine

John Korver works on the well-known illustration of Mike coming out of Tiger Stadium, 1960.

Courtesy University Relations

Mike III swats at something outside his cage.
Courtesy Joel Samuels

The Tiger Train, used to transport students from outlying parking lots to the center of campus, ran from 1963 until 1970.

alone. Meyer had another brush with disaster when Mike grabbed Meyer's foot with his paw. Meyer was sitting in the tiger house with his feet propped up against the cage bars when Mike decided to play with Meyer's leg. Of course after that Meyer decided he'd better keep his feet a bit further from the cage.

Joel Samuels reports that on at least three occasions, he accidentally entered the enclosure thinking that Mike was locked up when he wasn't. In two of Samuels' narrow escapes from the cage, Mike jumped up on the cage door just after the fleeing student closed it behind him. Bob Lank Jr., Mike's caretaker from 1968 to 1972, develops sweaty palms and a

Mike III greets visitors in 1964.

quickening pulse when he recalls the time he too found himself in the cage with Mike III. Lank was cleaning up in the outer enclosure when a bystander asked why Mike didn't attack him. He confidently replied, "Because of that gate." When the woman asked "What gate?" he turned to find that he had forgotten to lower the gate that locked Mike inside his tiger house. Fortunately, Mike was calmly eating his dinner and didn't notice the frightened student as he dashed out of the enclosure to

safety. Lank was terribly shaken up by the experience. In fact, he was so frightened that it took a few days for him to settle down.

Philip Aman, Mike's caretaker in the spring of 1972, recalls a similar experience. He had entered Mike's enclosure to clean up, forgetting to lock the tiger inside his house while the hungry cat ate his supper. Aman was in the process of hosing down the enclosure when he noticed his potentially fatal error. He realized that he had to make his escape before Mike noticed him. The only problem was having to cross in front of the open gate of Mike's house. Having to choose between a risky escape and certain danger once Mike finished his dinner, Aman made a dash for the outer gate. As he rushed by the open door, he startled Mike, who turned only in time to see the student reach safety. After composing himself, Aman dropped the gate, locking Mike in the house, and returned to his duties inside the enclosure.

Paul Marks Jr., Mike's caretaker from 1963 to 1965 recalls that once in the early sixties when LSU was to play Ole Miss, it was rumored that the Ole Miss fans were planning a caper the night before the game. It seems they planned to paint whatever they could find, including Mike III if possible, red and blue. The campus police encouraged Marks to spend the night guarding Mike's cage. That did not seem like the best idea to a student who liked his

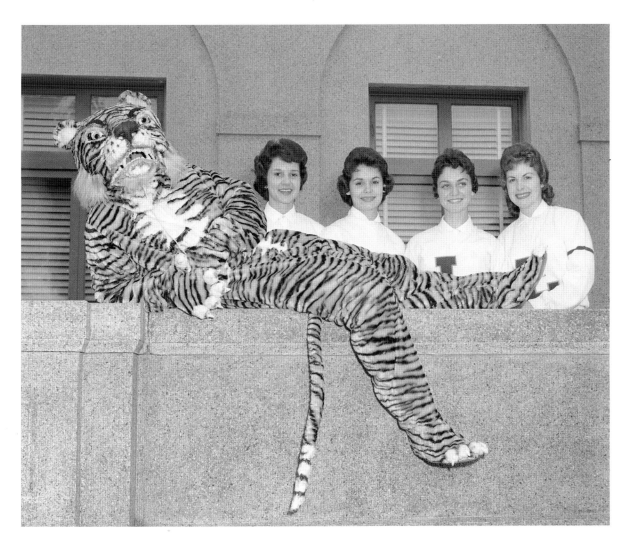

The new tiger suit is introduced in 1959.

Courtesy University Relatons

Alabama coach "Bear" Bryant gets friendly with Mike in this photo taken in 1981 at Legion field in Birmingham. Bryant was not so happy with Mike III's ability to roar on cue when he did so near the Alabama football players at an earlier time in Tiger Stadium.

Tim Statum

sleep. So Mike was loaded into his trailer for a trip to the home of Marks's parents. There he spent a peaceful night in a closed garage, safe from any would-be Picassos from Mississippi. And the student got his good night's sleep!

Because LSU competed in so many bowl games during the reign of Mike III, his caretakers have many stories to tell of their travels. Joel Samuels tells of taking Mike III to Dallas for the Cotton Bowl of 1966, when LSU was

pitted against the Razorbacks of Arkansas. Though a two-touchdown underdog, LSU won the game 14–7. Afterward, at the Cotton Bowl banquet, the governors of Louisiana, Arkansas, and Texas were deeply engrossed in conversation with one another. When Samuels was introduced as "the Tiger Man," all three governors stopped their conversation and turned their attention to him. Each was more interested in talking about Mike than in talking to one another. Samuels also recalls an LSU-Alabama game when Bear Bryant was the Alabama head coach. Samuels had a way of getting Mike to growl simply by saying, "Get 'em Mike." As the Alabama players gathered around the tiger trailer, Samuels quietly gave Mike the signal to growl. When Mike did so, it so unnerved the Alabama players that Coach Bryant took Samuels aside and gave him a stern lecture, advising him in no uncertain terms that he was not to upset his players like that. As far as we know, none of the other tigers growled on verbal cue.

For many years, the tiger trailer was usually pulled by a Ford Fairlane convertible provided by Richards Ford. The same dealership, now named Hollingsworth Richards Ford, is still among the local dealerships graciously providing vehicles for Mike's transport. Joel Samuels reports that in the 1960s, he would sometimes be loaned the next year's Ford model to pull the trailer. These models were so new that

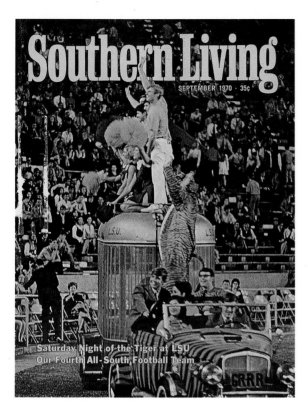

September 1970 issue of *Southern Living* features the roadster painted in a tiger motif.

1970 Southern Living, Inc. Reprinted with permission.

many fans were seeing them for the first time. In 1968, an LSU fan from Florida donated a roadster painted in a tiger motif. The car was used to tow the tiger trailer before the football games. Bob Lank Jr., Mike's caretaker at the time, reports that while the roadster was certainly beautiful, he was very disappointed at losing the convertible. He had been looking forward to using that car on the weekends when not pulling Mike. He says that the roadster was very difficult to maneuver within the stadium and would frequently overheat. After

the 1972 season, the tiger keepers retired the roadster and began using trucks to pull the trailer.

Mike III stopped traveling with the football team in 1972 when his trailer overturned on Highway 190 en route to a fund-raising event in Shreveport. Randy Kilgore was not driving on that trip but was along for the ride as Mike's student caretaker. He reports that the accident occurred because an incorrectly sized ball had been installed on the towing vehicle. When the trailer hit a bump in the highway, it

Cheerleaders dismount the trailer.

Trailer being pulled in Tiger Stadium by a Ford Fairlane convertible.

Courtesy Joel Samuels

Mike III in 1968.

bounced clear of the towing vehicle, ran into the median at forty-five miles per hour, flipped twice, and collided with a tractor-trailer rig. Amazingly, Mike escaped with only a small wound on one paw. Traffic backed up for miles. Police from seven different units arrived on the scene, along with a police helicopter. The trailer sustained so much damage that Mike had to be freed from it by cutting the door off with a torch. After that incident it was decided that a police escort should accompany all future tigers whenever they left campus. That policy remains in force to this day.

It was in 1976 that Dr. Sheldon Bivin of the LSU School of Veterinary Medicine was asked to take over as veterinarian for Mike III. Dr.

A 1970 illustration of Mike.
Courtesy Thomas Todd

Bivin was head of both the Division of Laboratory Animal Medicine and the exotic animal medicine service in the School of Veterinary Medicine. He was therefore the natural choice to become Mike's next veterinarian. This marked the formal transfer of responsibility for the tiger from the Athletic Department to a veterinarian. Mike was quite old at the time and was experiencing more frequent age-related health problems. These problems included painful, degenerative bone changes that made walking and even eating difficult. It was suggested by some that Mike be humanely put

to sleep, but others did not believe that was fitting for an LSU mascot, and so Mike lived on for a short while. It was during the latter part of Mike III's life that student attitudes toward keeping a tiger captive in a small enclosure began to change. Efforts were begun to provide Mike with a larger, more natural enclosure. Dr. Bivin and others suspected that while Mike III would probably not live long enough to see a new enclosure, future mascots would certainly benefit from an improved, more natural habitat.

Mike III served as LSU's mascot for eighteen years. During his lifetime LSU won the national championship in football (with a 7–0 win over Clemson) and three SEC champi-

Mike's home in 1975 when students began to raise money to enlarge and improve the 39-year-old cage.
Baton Rouge Advocate

Menacing Mike III in cage.

Courtesy Joel Samuels

onships (in 1958, 1961, 1970); the football team played thirteen bowl games, winning eight of them, and compiled a 142-50-7 record overall. Mike III died of pneumonia on Thursday, August 12, 1976, after the only losing season (5-6-0) of his lifetime. Dr. Bivin helped a local taxidermist remove the pelt. The body of the mascot was cremated, and the pelt was preserved and retained by the taxidermist. Contrary to what many people believe, the tiger on display for many years at a local restaurant in Baton Rouge is not Mike III. That tiger had been shot in the wild by a local hunter and donated to the School of Veterinary Medicine. After some of the veterinary faculty objected to the school having a stuffed

"Bengal Tiger"

The original of this etching of Mike III, produced for the Alumni Association, hangs in the Kent Anderson Room at the Lod Cook Alumni Center on the LSU campus.

Etching by Glenn Gore, 1973

animal which had been shot, the school donated the mount to the restaurant.

MIKE III'S STUDENT CARETAKERS

1958–59: Bill Levenson

1959–61: Douglas Davidson

1961–63: Alvin Meyer Jr.

1963–65: Paul Marks Jr.

1965–68: Joel Samuels

1968–72: Robert Lank Jr.

1972: Philip B. Aman

1972–76: Randy Kilgore

1976: Sonny Corley

Mike IV

Prather Warren, Universtiy Relations

Mike IV (1976–1990)

Mike IV was born at Busch Gardens in Tampa, Florida, on May 15, 1974. He was abandoned shortly after birth because his mother had health problems, and so he had to be hand raised. He was originally named Jerry. It was hoped that with all of his contact with people, he would be a tame tiger. However, that proved not to be the case. Thanks to a lot of work by the Tiger Booster Club and Jack Gilmore, Mike IV was donated to LSU on August 27, 1976, by August A. Busch III of Busch Gardens. After receiving a clean bill of health from Dr. Earl Schobert, veterinarian for Busch Gardens, the two-year-old, 450-pound tiger arrived at LSU on August 29, 1976.

Five years after his arrival, Mike spent the summer of 1981 at the Little Rock Zoo while

Mike's temporary home at the Little Rock Zoo while his cage in Baton Rouge was being expanded, September, 1981.

Baton Rouge Advocate

his enclosure was being expanded from four hundred to eleven hundred square feet. The expansion was completed at a cost of about $180,000. The new enclosure was actually sup-

61

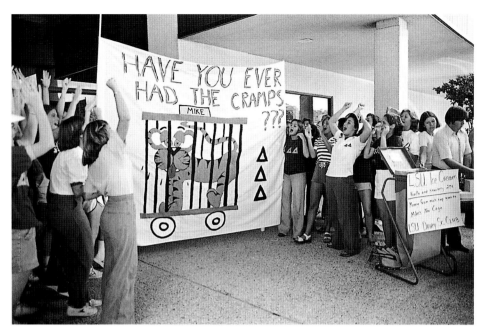

Delta Delta Delta fund-raising rally.

Mark Rayner

The expansion of the Mike's cage was finally done in 1981.

Gumbo

tunate that costs somehow increased so much from the time the first bids were received to the time the job was finished. Both Mike IV and Mike V could have benefitted greatly from a larger enclosure. The small size of the enclosure required keeping at least half of the flooring cement. This has been very hard on the tigers' feet.

Money for the expansion was raised from many sources. The LSU Student Government Association established the Friends of Mike committee, students attending LSU full time during the summer and fall of 1980 were assessed two dollars each at registration, the Athletic Department contributed, and LSU fans gave generously.

posed to be three times larger and was originally expected to cost about $30,000. However, construction cost overruns necessitated scaling down the size of the expansion. It was unfor-

Mike IV's expanded home.

Jim Zietz, Universtiy Relations

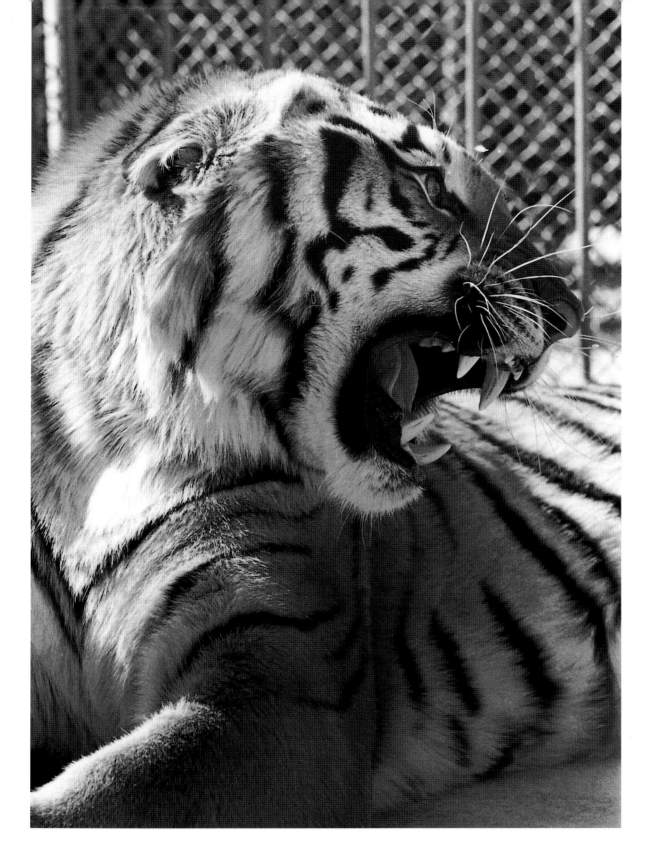

Mike IV roars.

Mark Rayner

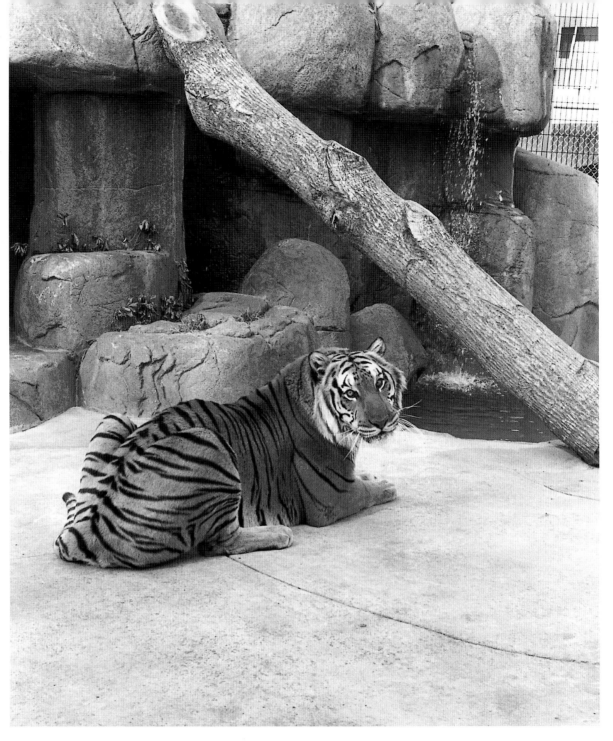

Mike IV in March 1982.

Courtesy Dr. Byron Garrity

When the expansion was completed and Mike IV returned from Little Rock, it took him some time to adjust to his higher style of living. Mike's keeper at the time, Byron Garrity, says that in his first few weeks in the refurbished surroundings, Mike was very wary of his swimming pool. After about a week, however, he came to love getting in his pool.

Mike also didn't know what to make of the grass that had been added to the enclosure. Being raised in captivity, Mike had never seen grass. He would walk around it and put his paw on it but wouldn't walk on it for several days. The grassy area would later be covered over during the reign of Mike V. Tiger urine is very caustic and created dead areas in the grass, quickly turning them to mud. It was feared that so much mud might promote foot infections.

One of the most famous incidents involv-

Mike IV in 1985 gets acquainted with Jim Zietz as he sits close by to photograph the famous tiger.

Prather Warren, University Relations

1983 close-up of Mike IV.

ing the tiger mascots occurred on November 28, 1981. At about 1:00 A.M., Dr. Bivin was sound asleep and ill with the flu when he got a call from the LSU police. "Mike's out," they said. "Mike who?" he asked. The police responded, "Mike the tiger. He's out in the middle of North Stadium Drive." How could Mike possibly have escaped? It seems that some pranksters had cut the chain to the outer door and the lock to the inner cage door, releasing the dangerous cat. Once he was convinced that this was not a joke, Dr. Bivin grabbed his rifle and rushed to campus. There he picked up tranquilizers and a dart gun. By the time he arrived on the scene, Mike was wandering around the north end of the Pete Maravich

One of the photographs from the session photographed above.

Jim Zietz, University Relations

Mike enjoys his pool.
Jim Zietz, University Relations

Assembly Center. He ended up in the Bernie Moore Track Stadium. Mike attacked a small tree along the way and appeared to be enjoying himself. Dr. Bivin joined a number of LSU police, including Wayne Ryland, who was the first officer to see the escapee. Police cars were placed at both ends of the stadium to keep Mike inside. They shone their lights toward him. Dr. Bivin bravely went out into the stadium with his tranquilizer pistol in one hand and his rifle in the other. The rifle was to pro-

tect himself and others from the tiger. Dr. Bivin managed to get downwind of Mike. The problem was, he had to be within about forty feet of the tiger to get a clean shot with the tranquilizer pistol. Bivin got as close as he could and got one dart into Mike. The big cat bolted and ran a short way and spun around to see where the dart came from. He spun around again and let out a growl and then a roar. He was mad! Within a few minutes the tranquilizer took effect and his back end be-

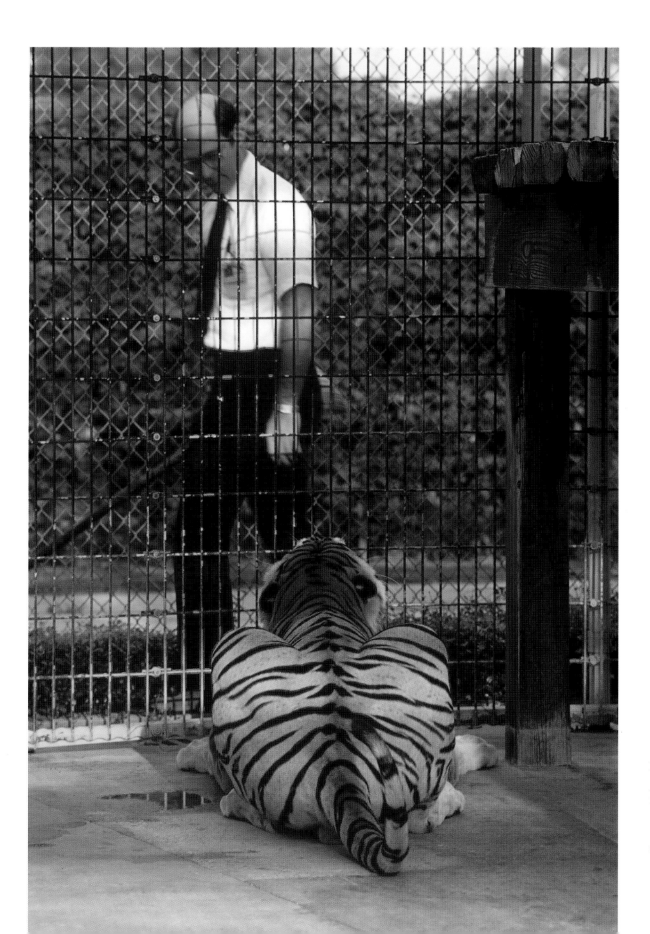

Dr. Bivin visits Mike IV.

Prather Warren, University Relations

67

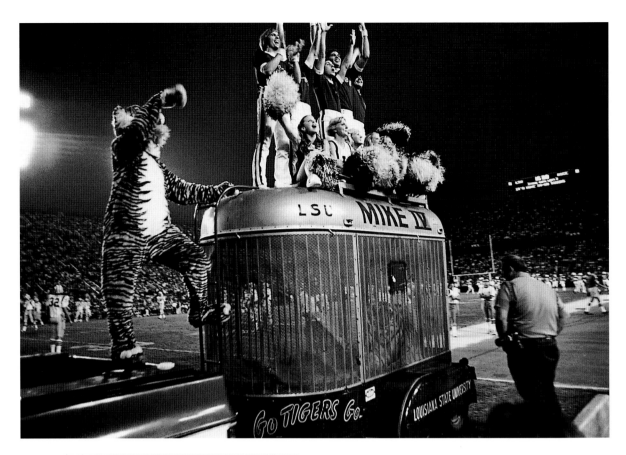

The cheerleaders and student mascot ride through Tiger Stadium with Mike IV on a Saturday night.

Mark Rayner

On the road again: Mike IV travels down I-110.

Mark Rayner

came uncoordinated. Dr. Bivin was able to get close enough to get a second dart into him. Mike bolted to the north end of the stadium and stood there for a while. Then his back end went down and he was up on only his front feet. He'd get up and then fall down. Finally, he must have decided it was all just too much trouble. He was down and growling but couldn't get up. That's when Dr. Bivin went right up to him and injected him with a third dose. When Mike was completely tranquilized, Dr. Bivin backed his truck up to him and finally coerced the campus police to help him lift Mike into the truck for the short ride back to his cage. Mike awoke the next morning with no ill effects. Shortly after Dr. Bivin returned home, his visiting father found him sitting in the kitchen reflecting on the whole episode. His father said, "Well, doggone, a good night's sleep sure does wonders for you. You sure look better this morning than you did last night." Dr. Bivin had a hard time convincing his father of what had happened during the night!

Throughout his life, Mike IV was a challenge to care for. Occasionally it was Mike who

Mike and his handler John D. DeVun, ca. 1985.

Baton Rouge Advocate

Mike IV

Mark Rayner

created a problem, but at other times trouble came from a variety of sources. There was the time when somebody turned a water mocassin loose in Mike's cage and the time Tulane stu-

The regal tiger sits on his
perch, ca. 1985.

Harry M. Cowgill

dents attempted to paint him green. In March 1978, Mike had a root canal performed by Dr. Bivin's dentist, Dr. M. E. Hoover. Mike had broken a canine tooth while trying to get hold of a tire outside his cage. Rather than sticking to the newly available, balanced, commercial diets formulated for zoo cats, Mike loved to bite off pieces of tires and garden hose, chew them up, and swallow them, and this was not the only time his taste for rubber caused a problem. Twice, in 1977 and again in 1990, he ate at least four feet of hose and required fairly intensive medical care for several days to help him pass all of the pieces. On Sept. 22, 1986,

Mike IV liked to chew leather and shows his love for football in this photograph.

Mike IV prowls around his home, ca. 1985.

Harry M. Cowgill

some Texas A&M Aggies threw a Valium-laced hotdog into his cage. Fortunately, it was retrieved before he could eat it. In addition to these episodes, he sometimes had wire cuts, intestinal problems, and sore feet. It is very difficult to provide medical care for a 480-pound man-eating patient with an "attitude."

When asked what closing Mike's cage for

Visitors gather around Mike's trailer at a School of Veterinary Medicine open house.

Jim Zietz, University Relations

the last time would mean to him, John DeVun, Mike IV's caretaker in 1986, replied, "I'll have mixed emotions. First, I can get a fair night's sleep knowing that every time my phone rings late at night it isn't someone telling me the tiger has gotten out. It has been something that crosses my mind every time the phone rings." But regretfully, he said, "I'll be sad to be ending something I'll likely never be able to do again. . . . I will be losing a friend."

Mike IV was quite a local traveler. Among other trips, he participated in Mardi Gras pa-

The tiger mascot shows off his pregame antics and his skill with a bow.

Jim Zietz, University Relations

rades in Thibodaux, Baton Rouge, and New Orleans. He accompanied LSU to the Sugar Bowl on January 1, 1985, where LSU played Nebraska. Unfortunately Mike's presence was not enough to put the Tigers over the top, and LSU was defeated by Nebraska, 28–10. In addition to his travels, Mike IV had a short but illustrious career as an actor, playing a tiger of course, in the movie *Everybody's All-American*, with costars Dennis Quaid and Jessica Lange. Although the movie was not a box-office smash, it was a good love story involving an LSU football star, and Mike appeared in many scenes.

One bizarre event in the life of Mike IV occurred in April 1988. The incident involved Moacyr Cezar, a disgruntled Brazilian who had come to Baton Rouge hoping to secure a job with the Athletic Department. Cezar took the keys from Jeff Perret, then Mike's student caretaker, and locked himself in the outer portion of the tiger enclosure. The man claimed

Mike IV, often photographed with his mouth open, seems to be expressing himself once again.

LSU Photograph Collection, RG A5000, LSU Archives, LSU Libraries, Baton Rouge

to have a gun and a bomb and threatened either to shoot or release Mike or explode the bomb. As campus and city police surrounded the tiger enclosure, he continued making threats for five hours. He finally surrendered after about two thousand students gathered around and started chanting, "Eat 'em up, Tigers, eat 'em up!" The man was afraid Mike might be turned loose on him. It turned out that his "gun" was a water pistol and his "bomb" was a sack of books. He was arrested and later returned to Brazil.

It was during the reign of Mike IV that a car tire was hung in the enclosure. Don Harris reports that one day while Mike was playing with his tire, some LSU football players came by to watch. Inquiring about Mike's strength,

they were told that without tying the end of a rope to the enclosure bars, there was no way to keep Mike from running off with the tire. Of course this brought forth challenges from the athletes. Harris locked Mike back in his tiger house, untied the tire from the bars, and had four or five linemen standing outside the bars hold onto the rope. When Harris released Mike from the tiger house, the mascot immediately came and took hold of the tire. The athletes pulled as hard as they could and were about to declare victory in the tug-of-war when Mike gave a couple of pulls and piled all of the men into the bars. As the players left, they asked if Harris could get Mike into the lineup for the next game, but Harris reminded them that eating the competition was against

NCAA rules. Six foot nine, 295-pound LSU defensive end Leonard Marshall, who later played for the New York Giants, had a similar tug-of-war demonstration of Mike IV's strength. This time the rope was looped through the top of the enclosure with Mike and the tire on one end and Marshall on the other. According to eyewitness accounts, Mike pulled down on the tire with such force that Marshall, who was pulling on his end, trying to lift the tire away from Mike, was himself lifted into the air! The other players who were watching were amazed at Mike's incredible strength. Unless one has seen it for oneself, it is difficult to imagine a full-grown tiger's strength.

Mike IV reigned for fourteen years at LSU and retired to the Baton Rouge Zoo in April 1990. Mike had developed a neurologic problem that resulted in mild lameness. In addition, he was getting along in years and was beginning to slow down. It became evident to Dr. Bivin that Mike IV needed less excitement in his life. The Baton Rouge Zoo graciously offered to take in the aging mascot. There he lived until his condition worsened and he became severely disabled. Mike IV was put to sleep on March 3, 1995. His life span of twenty

Prather Warren, University Relations

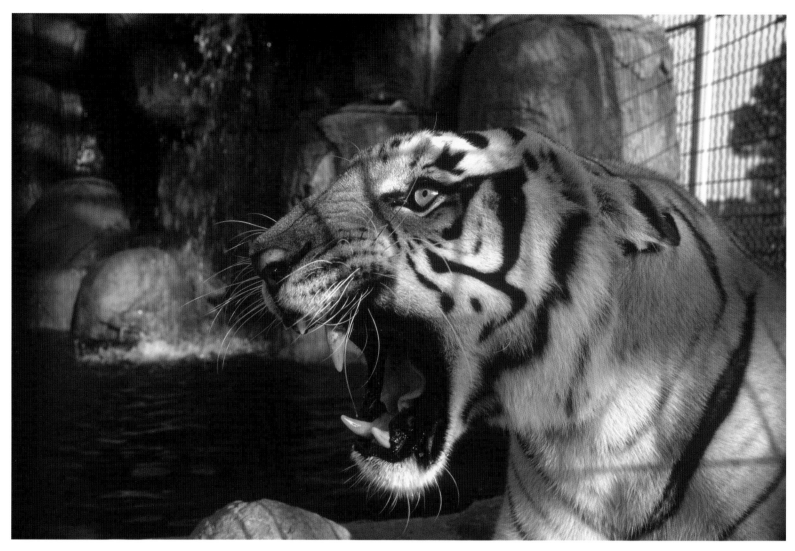

In this close-up of Mike IV you can see his much smaller upper right canine tooth.

Jim Zietz, University Relations

years, nine months, and eighteen days is considered extremely long for a captive tiger. It is one of the longest on record and the longest of any of the LSU mascots to date. The normal life span of a Bengal tiger is about eight to twelve years in the wild or around fourteen to eighteen years in captivity. After his death it was discovered that in addition to his neural problem, Mike had pneumonia and cancer of the thyroid. The cancer had spread into his chest and to his liver. That finding confirmed that putting Mike IV to sleep had been the most humane option. Like Mike III, Mike IV was cremated. Their ashes are in the LSU Sports Hall of Fame. When James H. Wharton, chancellor of LSU from 1981 to 1988, was asked about the significance of Mike to LSU, he eloquently stated, "Mike is LSU."

MIKE IV'S STUDENT CARETAKERS

1976–78: Sonny Corley

1978–80: Sonny Corley and
    Donald J. Harris Jr.

1980–82: W. Byron Garrity Jr.

1983–84: John R. Allender

1985–86: John D. DeVun

1987–88: Jeff Larisey

1989–90: Jeffrey Perret

Outgoing Mike IV *(left)* and incoming Mike V get acquainted before the elder tiger retired in 1990.

Harry M. Cowgill

C. C. Lockwood

Mike V (1990–Present)

Few people know it, but the title
"Mike V" was almost taken by a tiger other
than the current Mike V. In the fall of 1989, it
became evident that due to declining health,
Mike IV needed to be retired. A new tiger was
needed to take his place. George Felton, director of the Baton Rouge Zoo, found a two-and-
a-half-week-old cub at the Wild Wilderness
Safari in Arkansas. The cub was orphaned
when his mother died suddenly. Dr. Bivin ac-
quired the tiny cub and brought it to LSU. Because of his young age, the cub was cared for
around the clock. However, within a few
weeks, it was determined that the cub was
completely blind and would never see. The
cub had been born with cataracts. There was
nothing that could be done for him. Dr. Bivin

Fran Lupp plays with four-
and-a-half-month-old Mike
V and a toy tiger.
Baton Rouge Advocate

knew how difficult his life would be were he to
live. So the decision was made to humanely
put him to sleep.

Shortly afterward, the perfect cub was lo-

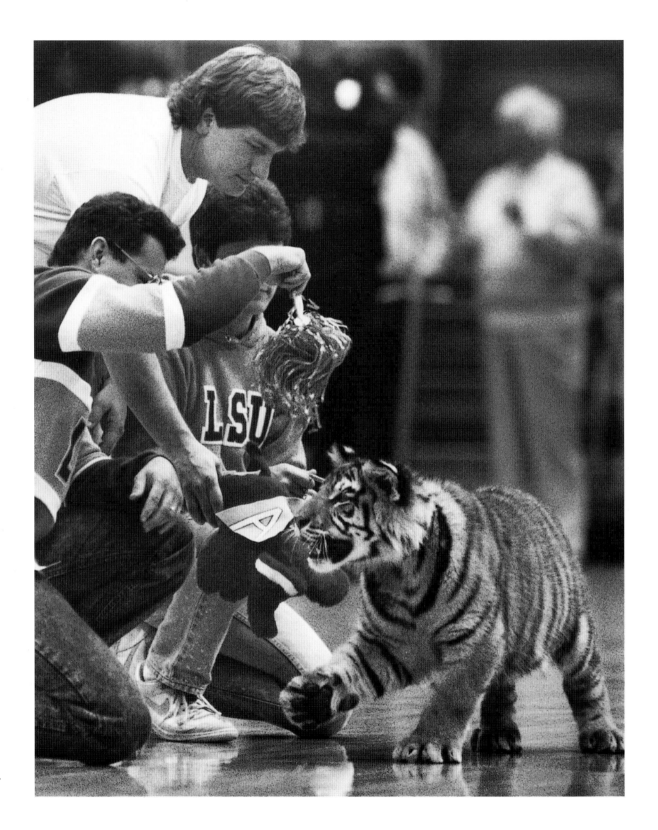

Mike V's introduction to the
LSU community was at the
LSU-Alabama basketball
game in February 1990.

Patrick Dennis, Baton Rouge Advocate

Dr. Bivin and others with a young Mike V.

Harry M. Cowgill

Chancelor William "Bud" Davis, William Jenkins (then dean of LSU's School of Veternary Medicine), Dr. Bivin, and William Coleman (then Vice Chancellor for Research) enjoy a day with the cub at the Penningon Center.

Harry M. Cowgill

cated. Born October 19, 1989, Mike V was given to LSU by Dr. Thomas and Caroline Atchison of the Animal House Zoological Park in Moulton, Alabama, on February 9, 1990. Charles J. Becker of the Tammany Tigers, an LSU booster group, put Dr. Bivin in touch with the Atchisons. Dr. Bivin traveled to Alabama to examine the four-month-old tiger cub and bring him back if he appeared suitable. The cub exceeded all of Bivin's expectations. Mike V was introduced to LSU fans at the LSU-Alabama basketball game in February 1990, formally "donated" by the Tammany Tigers. He was moved into his cage on April 30, 1990, and thus began his reign as Mike V. One of three cubs, Mike's name was originally

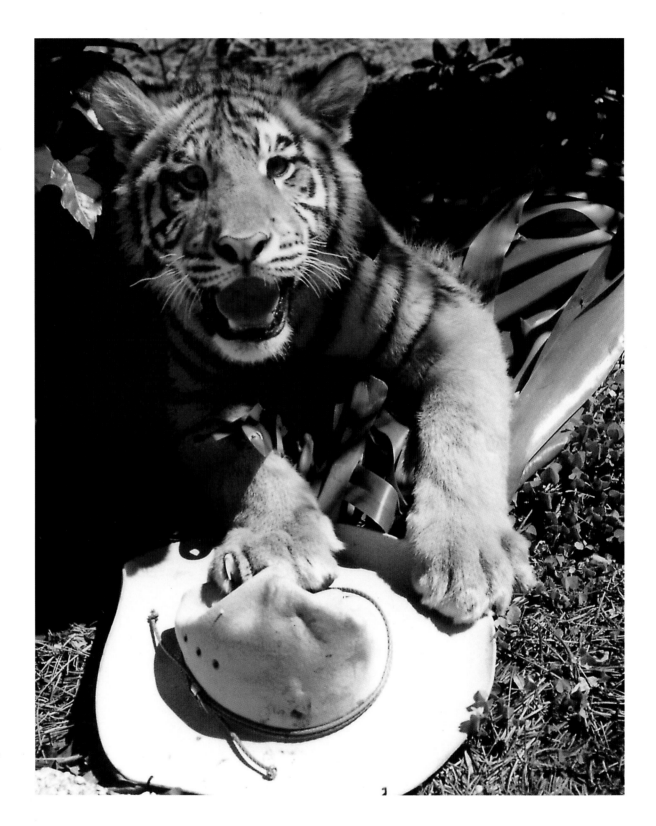

"Nobody touch my hat!": Mike V makes his first "kill" in the shrubbery on a visit to the vet school.

Pat Edwards

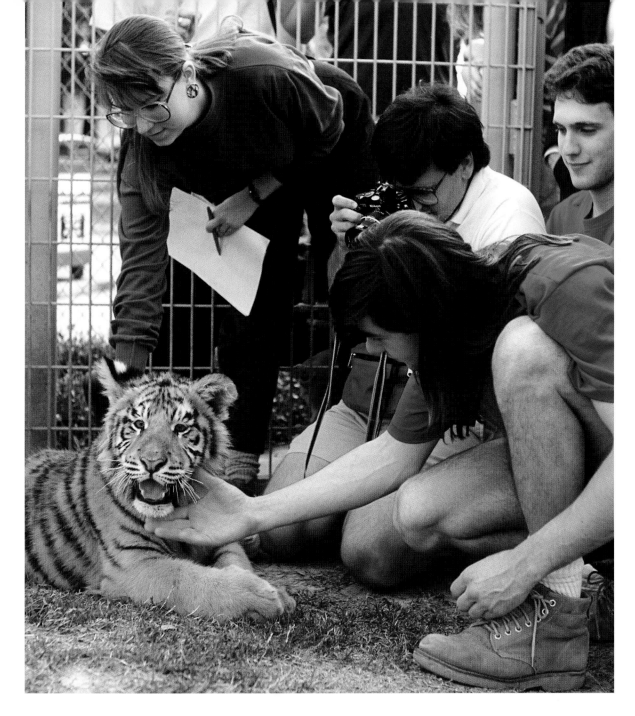

Mike V was hand raised and has been the easiest of the tigers to handle.

Jim Zietz, University Relations

"Stevie." Reportedly, his sister was in a movie about Mother Teresa, and his brother was sent to the Errol Flynn ranch in Aspen, Colorado, with plans to place him on display in a casino. Tom II, a brother of Mike's from a later litter,

serves as the proud mascot of the University of Memphis.

Of all the tigers that have served as LSU's mascot, Mike V has the best personality and has been the easiest to handle. This is in large

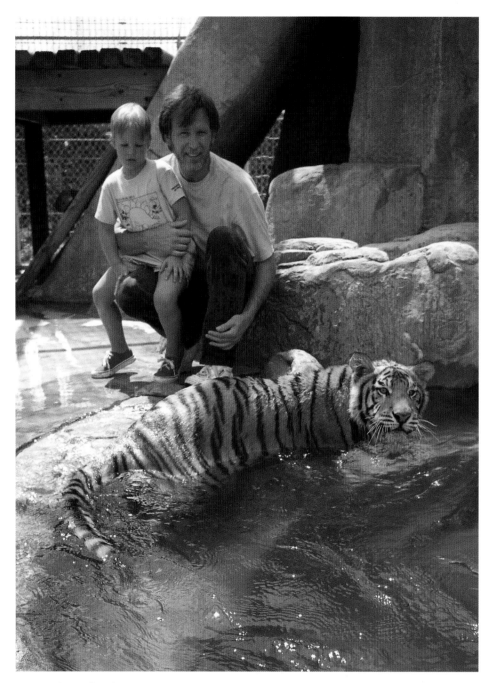

Lucas LeBoeuf and Harry Cowgill watch Mike as he swims in the pool within his enclosure.

Jim Zietz, University Relations

Mike V made his Tiger Stadium debut as the football team started its 97th season in the fall of 1990.

Baton Rouge Advocate

part because he came to LSU at such a young age and was hand raised by loving caretakers. In addition to the beneficial effects of hand-raising, Mike V seems to have been blessed with a friendlier, calmer disposition than most tigers. When he was not fully grown but was large enough to stand up and grasp people by the back of the neck with his jaws or dunk people under in his swimming pool, he would do so only playfully. But when his weight topped 250 pounds, the decision was made no longer to allow people into his enclosure with him. At that weight, Mike might accidentally hurt someone. And because he is a tiger and not a domestic animal, a day would probably come when his wild instincts would come out and he might attack someone.

Rollie Norris was the last student tiger caretaker to have contact with Mike with no bars between them. One day Norris took a photographer into Mike's enclosure. They thought Mike was safely locked on the other side of a gate. Much to their surprise, however, the gate was open! Mike came through the gate and ran right over the top of the terrified photographer. When he came back around for another "attack," Norris grabbed the photographer, threw him out of the enclosure, pushed Mike firmly on the nose, and got himself out before Mike decided to get aggressive. While it is unlikely that Mike would really have attacked with the intent to injure, one can't take chances with a 250-pound tiger. Norris' partner, Shelly Phillips, is the only woman ever to serve as a tiger caretaker. (Caretakers have usually been male because of the physical requirements of the job.) Phillips recalls the special opportunity she and Norris had to work with Mike V as a cub. To this day she is reluctant

Relaxing on the grass at the beginning of his reign as Mike V.

Harry M. Cowgill

The first time Mike was taken for a root canal was on May 13, 1997.

Harry M. Cowgill

even to visit Mike as an adult. She so enjoyed the contact with him when he was a cub that anything less leaves her with a melancholy feeling.

Mike V's first road trip was to the Superdome in December 1991 for a basketball game against Texas (which, with the help of Shaquille O'Neal, the Tigers won, 84–83). Apparently Mike was not very impressed with his trailer. He spent much of the return trip ripping the wire mesh off the back of it. Rollie Norris recalls that as a student, Shaquille O'Neal would often visit Mike at his cage. However, when given the opportunity to come inside for a closer look, O'Neal always de-

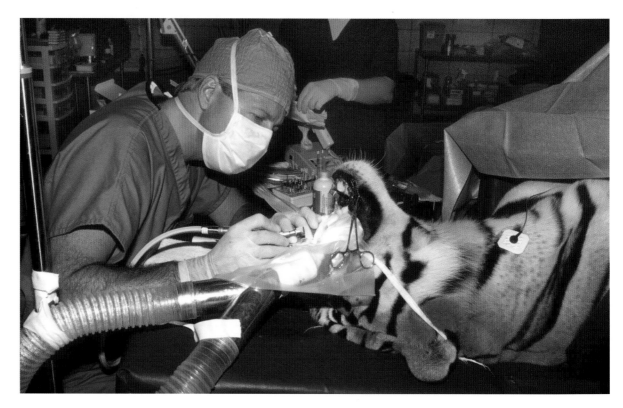

Dr. Alfred Stevens performs a second root canal on Mike on July 13, 2000.

Harry M. Cowgill

Mike enjoys an oxtail once a week, which helps keep his teeth clean.

C. C. Lockwood

clined. It seems he was content to observe Mike from well outside the enclosure.

Mike V has usually cooperated when it was time to load him into his trailer. In this regard, he has been easier to work with than his predecessors. To ensure Mike's well-being, however, off-campus travel has been greatly restricted. Whenever Mike V goes off campus, he is escorted by a uniformed LSU police officer. Even the LSU police officers who are not graduates of LSU consider it an honor to serve as Mike's escort. This is one of the many very important behind-the-scenes aspects of caring for a tiger mascot. Mike's veterinarians have always greatly appreciated the tremendous support provided by the LSU Police Department.

Like Mike IV before him, Mike V has presented his caretakers with a number of challenges. For example, in September 1996, Mike developed an overgrown and ingrown claw. As a result he became very lame and was completely unwilling for his new veterinarian, Dr. David Baker, to examine his foot. In April 1997, Mike had somehow broken his upper right canine tooth, exposing the pulp cavity. A root canal was performed on May 13, 1997, by a veterinary dentist from Michigan, Dr. Ben Colmery. Because a tiger's canine tooth is so

This grassy area would later be covered over because tiger urine is very caustic and created dead areas in the grass, quickly turning them to mud.

Harry M. Cowgill

long, special equipment is needed to extract the entire root. Dr. Colmery had the special equipment and had performed the procedure on several tigers. While Mike was asleep on the operating table, it was Dr. Baker who did the pacing while he waited anxiously for the surgery to end. Mike V is now the third LSU tiger to require a root canal. Dental problems are common in tigers and are, indirectly, the leading cause of death in wild tigers. As tigers age, their teeth become more brittle and are easily damaged or broken. In addition to Mike's

standard daily ration of five to ten pounds of a commercially prepared diet of meat, fish, soy, vegetables, vitamins, and minerals, he is given an oxtail once per week. The oxtail is an important part of Mike's dental health because it helps keep his teeth clean and maintains his jaw strength.

Providing Mike V with adequate environmental enrichment has been another challenge. This is important because it prevents boredom, which can lead to abnormal behavior. Mike's caretakers frequently come up with

Jim Zietz, University Relations (right)

new ways to keep him stimulated. For example, they hide his food in different places, construct artificial prey for him to tear apart, and place unusual scents in his enclosure. Matthew Wheelock recalls purchasing a kiddie pool for Mike. The plan was to get him used to the pool and then add fish. Surely Mike would love to watch the fish swim. Unfortunately, the plan broke down before any fish were added. It seems Mike didn't need the fish. He was happy just to destroy the pool! Pools of at least four different colors were tried in hopes of finding one that he wouldn't want to destroy. A suitable pool was never found, so the plan was abandoned. The experiment was not a total failure, however, because Mike certainly was entertained in the process!

On July 13, 2000, with the assistance of Dr. Gordon Pirie of the Baton Rouge Zoo, Dr. Baker removed a tumor from Mike's abdominal wall. Baker had noticed the enlargement a few days earlier while examining Mike. An ultrasound-guided biopsy confirmed that it was a tumor. While Drs. Baker and Pirie were removing the tumor, Dr. Kem Singletary and Dr. Alfred Stevens, a local practitioner with special expertise in veterinary dentistry, performed dental repairs. Stevens had assisted with the dental procedure in 1997 and now was equipped to perform the operation himself. The dental procedure was necessary because the unwilling patient had damaged a tooth during the ultrasound examination. After surgery, Mike V remained overnight at the School of Veterinary Medicine. Prior to returning him to his cage the next day, Matthew Wheelock and Kirk Mauer, Mike's veterinary student caretakers, drained his five-foot-deep pool. It was feared that if Mike were still affected at all by the anesthetics, he might fall into his pool and drown.

Most recently, in November 2001, Mike developed a temporary thyroid problem, which resulted in considerable weight loss and hormonal changes. Fortunately, however, the problem passed, and Mike returned to his normal, healthy condition. As Mike ages, it is anticipated that medical problems will become

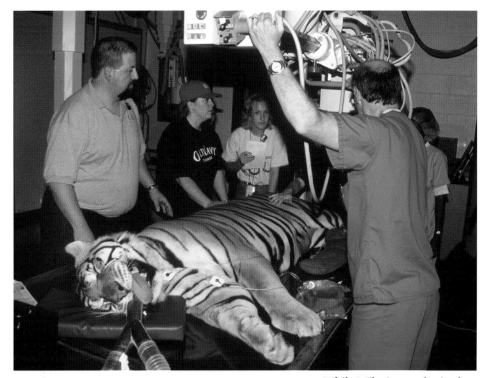

While Mike is anesthetized, technicians at the School of Veterinary Medicine take x-rays of his hips.

Harry M. Cowgill

Dr. David Baker *(right),* assisted by Dr. Gordon Pirie of the Baton Rouge Zoo, removes a tumor from Mike's abdominal wall.

Harry M. Cowgill

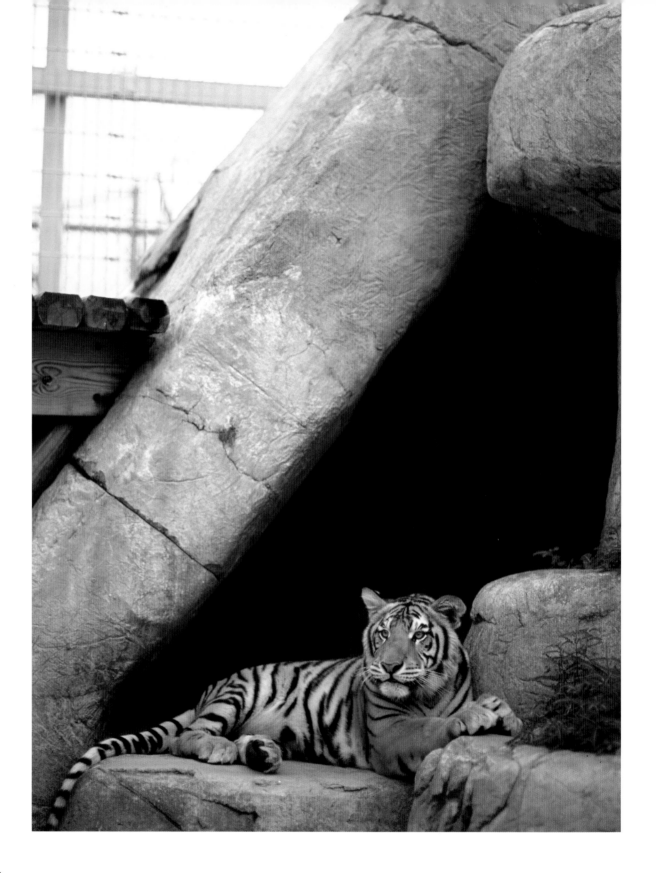

Mike sits in the shade and out of the heat as much as possible.

Harry M. Cowgill

more common. In that regard he is certainly like the rest of us. However, one can imagine the difficulty in providing excellent medical care for an aging animal that prefers not to be handled by his doctor. When Mike V was younger, most minor medical procedures were performed without the use of sedatives or anesthetics. But there is some risk in even temporarily confining Mike in his metal "squeeze chute" while a physical examination is performed or blood samples are collected. So as Mike V has aged, Dr. Baker has begun sedating him when medical procedures are necessary.

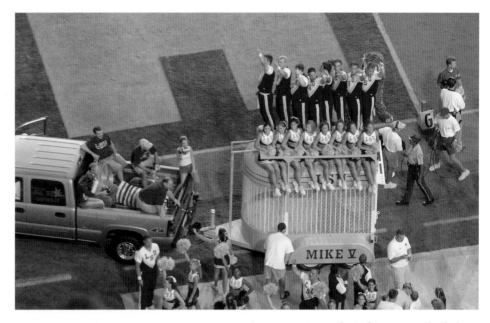

Mike in his new trailer helps stir the fan frenzy before a football game.

Jim Zietz, University Relations

The tiger trailer received a fresh coat of paint from Troy LeBlanc, seen here standing with the trailer.

Philip Cancilleri

It is the mascot in the tiger suit that, simply by walking up to Mike's trailer, gets the current Mike to roar before a football game.

By September 1997, the trailer used to transport all tigers since Mike II had worn out, after forty years of use. A new trailer was clearly needed to transport Mike V safely. A beautiful new trailer was graciously donated to LSU by Doug Guidroz and Rick Vallet, owners

of Central Hitch and Equipment in Baton Rouge. The expert trailer manufacturers had already constructed a number of high-quality trailers for the School of Veterinary Medicine. Dr. Baker therefore felt confident that the sturdy new tiger taxi would serve Mike V well into the future. A contest was held to allow the public to suggest the color scheme for the new trailer. Some wild designs were submitted. The winning design was drawn by Al Carter, and the new trailer was painted beautiful LSU gold with purple lettering. Thanks to a lot of hard work by the crew of Central Hitch and Equipment over the Labor Day weekend, the new trailer was ready in time for the home opener against Texas–El Paso on September 6, 1997. One need only imagine the dangers of being stranded with a broken-down trailer and a 400-pound tiger to appreciate the importance of a sturdy trailer for the safety of Mike and his handlers.

On January 1, 2002, Mike V once again ventured to the Superdome in New Orleans, this time to support the football team in its game against the University of Illinois in the Nokia Sugar Bowl. Unusually cold temperatures had been predicted for the week, and for once the forecasters turned out to be right. To protect Mike from the cold, his trailer was bedded deeply with straw, a custom-made cover was secured to the trailer, and the back was closed up with plywood sheets modified

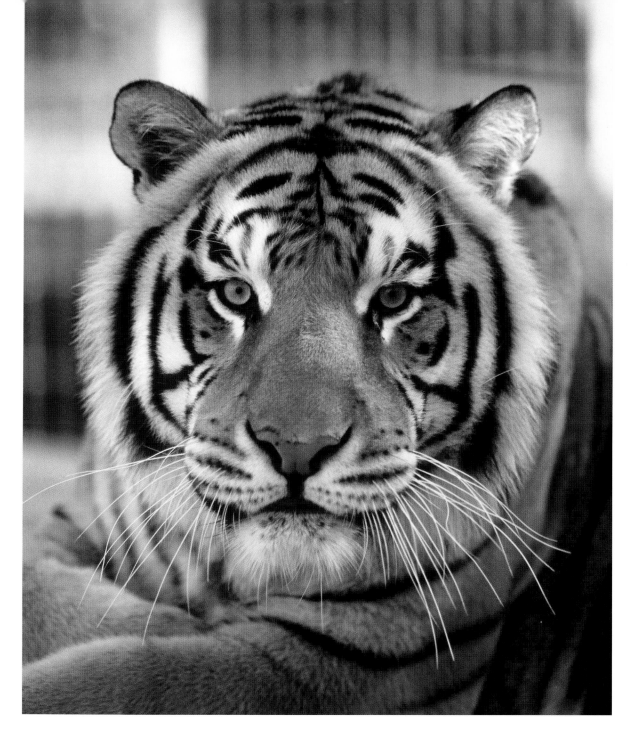

A pensive Mike.

Jim Zietz, University Relations

by Dr. Baker's eleven-year-old son, Martin. Dr. Baker even took a test ride in the trailer to make sure there were no chilling drafts coming in. Mike was accompanied by Dr. Baker and his veterinary student caretakers, Matthew Wheelock and Kirk Mauer, along with three guests. In addition, the LSU police sent along an officer in a squad car as an escort. Towing

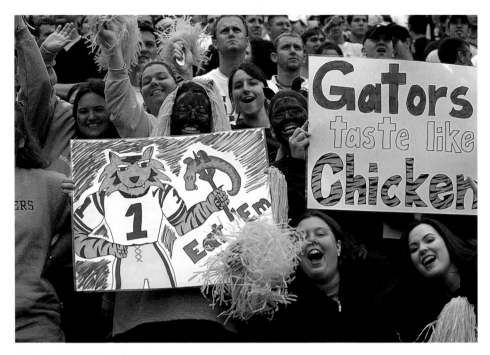

These football fans show their love for Mike and Tiger football.

C. C. Lockwood

power was graciously provided by Hollingsworth Richards Ford. Shortly after the group left Baton Rouge, freezing rain began to fall. Mike stayed for the first half of what was turning into a very long game. Not wanting to risk being involved in an accident if the roads froze, the tiger team elected to leave ahead of the crowd, which proved to be a wise decision. It snowed nearly all the way back to LSU. Mike reached the campus just as the game was ending in a 48–34 victory for the Tigers. Mike had enjoyed a long and eventful day, but rather than going directly into his house to rest, Mike first investigated the soft, cold, white powder

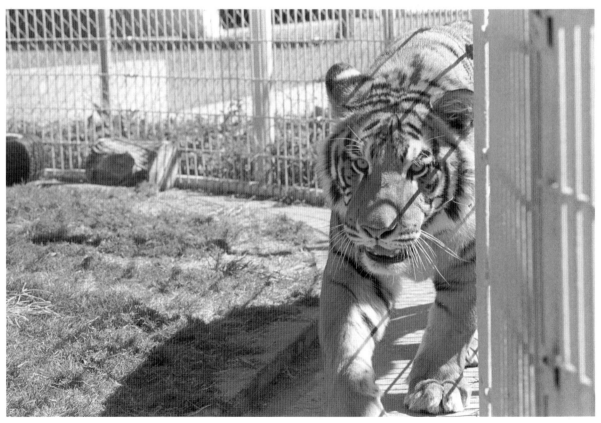

Pacing the cage.

Prather Warren, University Relations

98

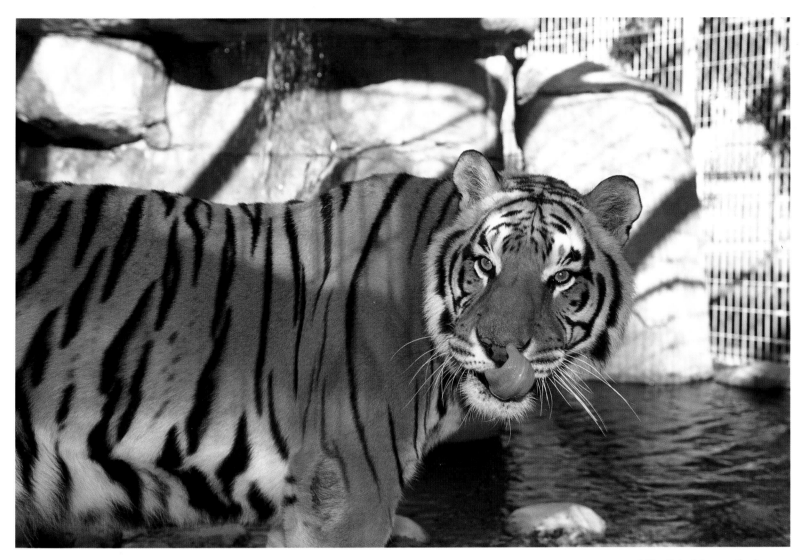

Mike licks his mouth clean after enjoying a good snack.

C. C. Lockwood

that had coated his entire enclosure. This was probably Mike's first experience with snow. He cautiously smelled it, tasted it, pawed at it, and slipped on it. After several minutes of investigating this new substance, he lost interest and retired to his warm house for a good night's sleep.

Anyone who has been involved in the care of the tigers has countless stories to tell of Mike's impact on people, but two stories in particular come to mind. The first occurred on October 19, 1997, Mike V's eighth birthday. Dr. Baker arrived at Mike's enclosure to find a young girl in an LSU cheerleader's costume tying a birthday card to the fence of Mike's enclosure. When Dr. Baker asked her about it, she told him that she and Mike V shared the same birthday. She too was eight years old. She

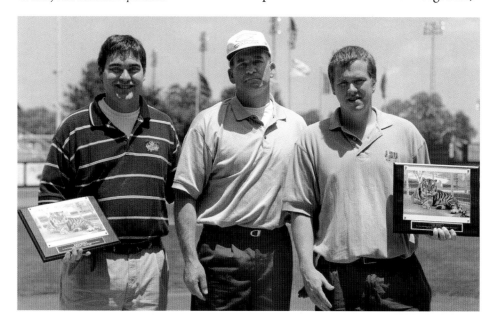

The changing of the guard: Steve Eastman and Leath Harper *(back)* take over the role of Mike's caretakers from David Webre and Shane Parker *(front)* in the spring of 1998.

Dr. Baker presents plaques to Matthew Wheelock *(left)* and Kirk Mauer in May 2002, thanking them for caring for Mike V.

Courtesy LSU Athletic Department

said that every year her grandmother brought her to Mike's house so she could leave him a birthday card and wish him well. Dr. Baker was so touched by her devotion to Mike that he took a picture of the two of them together, separated only by the fence. No doubt the little girl will cherish that photograph. She may someday come to LSU as a student, and she will very likely go through her adult life sensitive to the endangered natural world with which we share this planet. The second story involves a friend of Dr. Baker's whose mother was dying. As a small token of his appreciation for all she had done for him, the friend wrote down sixty acts his mother had performed for which he was very thankful. He had these professionally inscribed by a calligrapher, matted, and framed, and he presented the gift to his mother, who was then in the hospital. Toward the top of the list was written, "Thank you for taking me to see Mike the tiger." The Sunday afternoon visits to see Mike his mother had treated him to as a young boy had in some small way strengthened the special bond between them.

MIKE V'S STUDENT CARETAKERS

1990: Jeffrey Perret

1990–92: Rollie Norris and Shelly Phillips

1992–94: Jeffery Artall and Mark Gentry

1994–96: Lance Hidalgo and Randolph Hayes

1996–98: L. Shane Parker and David B. Webre

1998–2000: Leath Harper Jr. and Stephen Eastman

2000–2002: Matthew Wheelock and Kirk Mauer

2002 to present: Kevin Bankston and Blake Tunnard

All About Tigers

Many ask, "What are the advantages of keeping a Bengal tiger mascot?" This is a very good question. Some might quickly respond that maintaining the great Tiger tradition is reason enough. To many, Mike the Tiger is a unique and rousing symbol of the university and represents all that is good about LSU. But Mike is more than a symbol of a great university. He represents all tigers of the world. Indeed, he represents all the endangered animals with which we share this planet. In this respect, Mike provides an excellent and unparalleled opportunity to educate students, staff, faculty, and visitors of the plight of the world's endangered animals. Education is the primary function of the university. It is fitting that LSU use every opportunity, including our beloved mascot, to educate and thereby serve as a positive force in our community and the world.

SOME COMMON QUESTIONS

People are naturally curious about tigers. Their beauty and power have intrigued people throughout history. The tiger has a major place in some of the world's great religions. It is not by accident that the tiger is the most written about animal in Asia. Fascination with tigers is also evident on the LSU campus. It is estimated that Mike receives roughly 100,000 visitors per year. The following are some of the questions people most commonly ask about Mike and other tigers.

How many different kinds of tigers are there?

Surprisingly, there is no simple and definitive answer to this question. Traditionally, conservationists have recognized five extant subspecies of tigers based on geographical location and differences in appearance. Physical features used to characterize subspecies include size, color, number and pattern of stripes, and skull size. More recently, scientists have begun conducting molecular DNA studies to determine the true relatedness of different populations of tigers. Genetic analyses suggest that there are no true subspecies and that tigers only appear different because of adaptations to local environments. This view may eventually result in a shift away from efforts to preserve subspecies and toward a greater focus on maintaining the great variation within the tiger population. For now, we will retain the historical view, and will assume that there are five living subspecies. In addition to the living subspecies, three subspecies have become extinct. (Despite its popular name, the long-extinct sabertooth tiger was not really a tiger.) The living tigers include:

LSU's Mike V is an example of a Bengal tiger *(Panthera tigris tigris).*

C. C. Lockwood

102

Bengal *(Panthera tigris tigris)*. Also known as the Royal Bengal or Indian tiger, this is the least endangered subspecies of tigers. This subspecies includes tigers with white or, less commonly, black color mutations. The current natural range of the Bengal tiger includes areas of India, Nepal, Bangladesh, Bhutan, and northwest Myanmar. There are probably about three to five thousand wild Bengal tigers. Most of them live in protected areas.

Indochinese *(Panthera tigris corbetti)*. The natural range of this subspecies comprises most of the jungles of southern Asia, including southern China, Myanmar, Thailand, Vietnam, Laos, Cambodia, and Malaysia. It is estimated that approximately 2,000–3,500 wild Indochinese tigers live within their natural range.

Siberian *(Panthera tigris altaica)*. Also called the Amur, Manchurian, or Northeast China tiger, the Siberian is the largest tiger. The heaviest Siberian tiger weighed in at over a thousand pounds! This subspecies' current range is wooded areas of northeast China and southeast Russia. The estimated wild population is between two hundred and four hundred.

South China *(Panthera tigris amoyensis)*. Also known as the Chinese or Amoy tiger, the South China tiger has the fewest stripes. The current range of the South China tiger

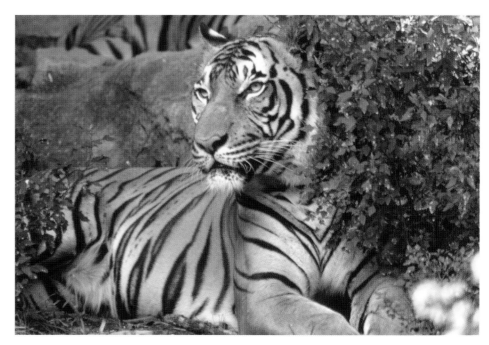

Indochinese *(Panthera tigris corbetti)*.

Barbara Von Hoffmann / Animals, Animals

The largest tiger is the Siberian *(Panthera tigris altaica)*.

Mark Stouffer / Animals, Animals

The South China tiger *(Panthera tigris amoyensis)* has the fewest stripes and the smallest population in the wild.

Courtesy Save China Tigers

is limited to wooded areas of eastern China. There may be less than fifty of these tigers remaining in the wild. They are spread out over twenty-one tiger reserves, making it difficult for them to find one another.

Sumatran *(Panthera tigris sumatrae)*. At about 250 pounds, the Sumatran tiger is the smallest of living tigers. The Sumatran tiger also has the most pronounced "ruff," or collar of hair around the head. This tiger inhabits the jungles of Indonesia (Sumatra). It is estimated that about five to six hundred Sumatran tigers live in the wild,

The Sumatran *(Panthera tigris sumatrae)* is the smallest of the living tigers.

C. C. Lockwood

104

with all but about one hundred of them living in five national parks in Indonesia. The remainder live in unprotected areas.

The following subspecies of tigers are extinct:

Balinese *(Panthera tigris balica).* The Balinese tiger was the smallest of the tigers, weighing only about two hundred pounds. This tiger occupied the Bali islands of Indonesia. It was declared extinct in 1970 but had not been seen since 1937.

Javan *(Panthera tigris sondaica).* The Javan tiger occupied the islands of Javan Indonesia. The Javan tiger was declared extinct in 1972.

Caspian *(Panthera tigris virgata).* A relatively large tiger at about 530 pounds, the Caspian tiger roamed the wooded areas of northern Afghanistan, northern Iran, eastern Turkey, western Mongolia, and southern Russia. It was declared extinct in 1980 but had not been seen for many years before that.

Where do tigers live?

Tigers live in wooded areas that range from tall grasslands with few trees to thick forests to nearly impenetrable jungles. The amount of territory claimed by a male tiger is determined primarily by two things: the abundance of food and, less importantly, the abundance of female tigers. In India, where prey is abundant, a male's territory may be as small as eight square miles. At the other extreme, in Siberia, where prey is scarce, a male tiger may require over one hundred square miles. Typically a tiger's territory is about twenty to thirty square miles. Other environmental factors such as the presence of water, also affect territory size. Tigers are excellent swimmers, easily crossing bodies of water up to five miles across.

Why does Mike live alone?

Many people think that Mike needs a mate. They assume that he is lonely without another tiger. However, neither of those assumptions is true. Because of their method of hunting and capturing prey, wild tigers live alone for most of their adult lives. Tigers stalk their prey, often through dense forest or brush. A tiger will approach to within fifty to one hundred feet of its prey before making a short charge, usually from behind. So for tigers, two's a crowd. Another tiger might frighten off the prey, and both would go hungry. Even alone, tigers fail to capture their prey more often than they succeed. Solitary living is instinctive for tigers, and simply keeping them in captivity will not change those instincts. It can be very dangerous to introduce one adult tiger to another. There would certainly be a terrible fight, and if one were a female, she would

TIGER HABITAT

Based on information from the Tiger Information Center

Map by Tara St.Romain

HISTORICAL RANGES

- Bengal tiger
- South China tiger
- Indochinese tiger
- Siberian tiger
- Sumatran tiger

CURRENT RANGES

- Bengal tiger
- South China tiger
- Indochinese tiger
- Siberian tiger
- Sumatran tiger

EXTINCT RANGES

- Caspian tiger
- Java tiger
- Bali tiger

probably be killed. When Mike I was taken to the R. M. Taylor Zoo in Jackson, Mississippi, in 1945 to be mated to a female tiger, he had to return to LSU still a bachelor. After Mike and his intended mate had had several months of fence line contact, officials felt that the tigers still appeared too aggressive toward one another to risk putting them together.

How do tigers reproduce?

If tigers are solitary animals, how do we get more tigers? While tigers live alone most of the time, they do get together for breeding. In fact, the territories of two or more females are often within the territory of a male, though they rarely encounter one another. The territories of two males, however, never overlap. Although tigers are solitary, they form a complex society. They leave scent markings with urine and feces and with glands on their paws. They also put scratches on trees and roll on the ground to let other tigers know of their presence. In these ways tigers remind one another of their territorial boundaries. Even Mike leaves these markings, though he lives alone. Many unsuspecting visitors, standing a little too close to his fence, have been marked as Mike's "territory"! When the female tiger is ready to mate, she will seek out and become very friendly toward the male. Tigers may breed hundreds of times over the course of about a week—about every fifteen minutes

when the female is at her peak of receptivity.

The gestation period is about 102 days. Cubs weigh about two pounds when born. While up to five cubs may be born in one litter, two or three is more common. Females typically produce a litter every two to three years. Cubs are entirely dependent on their mother for the first six months of life. Then she begins to teach them to hunt for themselves. By about eighteen months they can go off on their own and fend for themselves. The young females tend to remain with their mothers longer than the young males. Both sexes reach reproductive maturity at around three years of age. Of every one hundred tigers born, only about twenty will survive to reproduce.

When fully grown, male tigers usually weigh about four to five hundred pounds, depending on their subspecies. Female tigers generally weigh about one hundred pounds less. The natural life span of a wild tiger is usually only about eight to twelve years, with a maximum of about fifteen years. Diseases, injuries, poaching, and starvation exact a heavy toll, especially on males. In captivity, tigers do not encounter these threats, so they generally live longer. Most tigers in captivity live about fourteen to eighteen years. Except for Mike II, the LSU tigers have enjoyed remarkably long and healthy lives. Three of the LSU tigers lived over nineteen years.

What do tigers eat?

Tigers will eat almost anything that moves. Their favorite foods are deer and wild pigs, though they can kill animals as large as water buffalo. In fact, tigers are the only predators of large hoofed animals in Asia. These animals are so important to the survival of the tiger that where they have disappeared, the tiger has soon followed. Tigers eat ten to fifteen pounds of food at a time, staying with the kill until they have eaten it all. A male will make about fifty major kills per year, and a breeding female will make up to around seventy. Tigers eat nearly the whole carcass, not just the muscle meat. In this way they obtain all the nutrients they need. Long ago, tigers in captivity were fed only muscle meat. As they aged, this diet often resulted in the development of arthritis. Because Mike V does not have the physical requirements of a wild tiger, he is fed five to ten pounds of food per day and is usually fasted one day per week. Mike eats a balanced, commercially prepared diet made especially for large cats. It is the consistency of hamburger but is made of horsemeat or beef, fish, vitamins, minerals, and vegetables. Mike's diet is supplemented with extra vitamins. In addition, Mike is given an oxtail once per week to help keep his teeth clean, maintain jaw strength, and provide environmental enrichment.

How can we tell one tiger from another?

At first glance, all tigers may appear to look alike. However, tigers can be identified by their stripe patterns. No two tigers have exactly the same striping, just as no two humans have the same fingerprints. Nobody knows why tigers have stripes. It is probably to conceal them from their prey. The Sumatran tiger has the most stripes, and the South China tiger has the least. It is a common misconception that tigers can be reliably identified by their footprints, or pug marks, since pug marks change over time. As a tiger gains or loses weight, grows, experiences injuries to the foot pads, and ages, the marks change.

Where will the next Mike come from?

While there has been a terrible loss of tigers from the wild, there seems to be no shortage of tigers in captivity. It is estimated that there may be up to fifteen thousand captive tigers in the United States alone, more than twice the number of wild tigers in the world. But if there are so many tigers in captivity, why does LSU need a tiger? First, the vast majority of captive tigers are privately owned and not available for viewing by the public. Consequently they provide no educational benefit. An important reason for having "Mike" is the educational benefit that comes from having over 100,000 people per year visit him. He is an individual tiger, but he also represents all tigers, as well as all endangered animals. Second, many of the tigers in the United States are owned illegally. An alarming number of "sportsmen" are willing to pay two thousand to twenty thousand dollars to "hunt" a tiger. This often involves shooting a tiger in a fenced area or even in a cage. This gruesome practice is surprisingly common. It is estimated that there are over a thousand "canned hunt" providers in the United States alone. It is hoped that those who visit Mike will gain a greater appreciation of tigers and will help to combat the inhumane killing of tigers in such "hunts."

TIGER CONSERVATION

As recently as 1900, up to about 100,000 tigers roamed the woods and jungles of Asia. Subspecies of tigers lived as far west as Turkey and the Caspian Sea. They ranged as far north as southeastern Russia and as far south as the islands of Indonesia. Today it is thought that less than seven thousand tigers remain in the wild. However, the tiger is a very difficult animal to count, and it is feared that the actual number may be lower. The remaining wild tigers are all found scattered among 160 isolated populations, or tiger conservation units. Loss of habitat, inadequate food sources, poaching, and population fragmentation have decimated wild tiger populations. The natural range of tigers has declined as huge tracts of forest have been cleared for timber or farming. Only relatively small patches of forest remain. With the loss of habitat and the hunting of wild game for human consumption, once abundant prey has also become much harder to find. Loss of prey is the single most important factor in the reduction in tiger populations. Lack of natural prey causes tigers to kill livestock and occasionally humans, resulting in the killing of tigers by local villagers. In addition to these challenges, tigers are poached for their body parts, which are superstitiously believed to have medicinal value. For example, the eyeballs are thought to cure epilepsy; the whiskers, toothaches; the brain, laziness and pimples; the tail, skin diseases; and the bones are believed to cure rheumatism, weakness, and paralysis. Lastly, fragmentation of habitat likewise separates and fragments tiger populations. The remaining tigers are so spread out that they cannot find one another for breeding or they repeatedly breed within a small group, resulting in a weakened gene pool.

There is no doubt that like many other animal species, the tiger is in grave danger of extinction in the wild. Yet there are some exciting and encouraging efforts under way to save the tiger in its natural habitat and to establish genetically healthy captive breeding populations of each of the five tiger subspecies. One of the most important advances in tiger conservation has been the establishment of a species survival plan (SSP) for tigers. An SSP is a cooperative management program administered by the American Zoo and Aquarium Association (AZA) with input from scholarly conservation organizations. A number of SSPs have been developed to conserve wild populations of various endangered species, including the tiger. The programs seek to establish and oversee healthy captive stocks of endangered animals, mostly in the United States. These animals serve as reservoirs of genetic material that, under tightly controlled guidelines, can be used to reestablish or revitalize wild populations. Once an SSP has been established, selected American zoos holding the particular animal species work together to form a master plan for managing the species. The master plan includes recommendations concerning mate selection, shipment of individual animals for breeding purposes, and support for other programs designed to protect the species in the wild. The tiger SSP was the first SSP established by the AZA. In 1988, the tiger SSP master plan made recommendations concerning the numbers of each of the tiger subspecies that should be held in captivity. In 1992, the plan was modified to include about a hundred tigers from each subspecies. These tigers are to be housed in participating zoos across North

America. The plan also called for cooperation with other regional programs, such as those in Europe, India, and Southeast Asia.

In addition to the AZA's tiger SSP, international efforts are under way to save the tiger. Among the most significant is the Tiger Global Animal Survival Plan (GASP). The Tiger GASP has been organized to provide a strategic framework for information sharing and to make recommendations concerning tiger management on an international level. The Tiger GASP committee has identified several areas of scientific study deemed critical to survival of the tiger, including molecular DNA studies, population and habitat viability studies, geographic information systems for assessing satellite images of tiger rangeland, and captive management programs. Several ancillary scientific programs are also advancing the cause of tiger conservation in the areas of contraception, in vitro fertilization, and genome banking.

Over the past thirty years, many national and international laws, guidelines, and regulations have been developed to protect the tiger. The most important international agreement protecting tigers from poaching is the Convention on International Trade in Endangered Species of Wild Fauna and Flora (CITES). The CITES bans international trade in tigers and tiger body parts. Currently, 145 countries are signatories to the CITES agreement, which requires member countries to actively enforce efforts to prevent illegal trade practices. Unfortunately, enforcement of CITES policies is spotty, with several signatory countries not doing all that they should to protect tigers and prohibit trade in tiger parts. Violations of CITES policies have occasionally resulted in application of trade sanctions against wayward countries. These punitive steps have generally improved compliance.

Regional conservation efforts have also been organized in range countries, where tigers are found in the wild. The Global Tiger Forum is a regional agreement initiated in India in 1994. The forum includes representatives of several range countries and seeks to eliminate trade in tiger parts, support tiger habitats, and promote training and research in tiger conservation. Support for these programs has also come from nonrange countries. In 1999, the United Kingdom became the first non-tiger-range country to join the Tiger Global Forum. Several local governments in Asia have also enacted laws to protect the tiger. Unfortunately, enforcement of these laws has been inconsistent.

In the United States, there are several federal laws, principles, and regulations that proscribe the conditions under which tigers may be kept and that prohibit trading in tigers and tiger parts. The Animal Welfare Act, administered by the United States Department of Agriculture (USDA), describes the housing, transportation, and medical requirements of institutional or private ownership of tigers, as well as many other species of exotic animals. USDA veterinarians regularly inspect facilities housing tigers and evaluate the standard operating procedures used to care for them. The Rhinoceros and Tiger Conservation Act of 1998 provides funding for programs designed to support and enhance wild tiger populations. The Rhino and Tiger Product Labeling Act of 1998 prohibits trade in tigers and tiger parts and seeks to disrupt the flow of tiger parts into the United States. In addition to these federal efforts, at least thirty-two states have enacted laws regulating or banning trade in tigers. More importantly, many states have enacted laws that specifically target canned tiger hunts.

Tiger conservation is at a crossroads. The fate of the tiger will be determined within the next generation. For the tiger to be saved, more cooperation is needed between national and international governing bodies. These groups must no longer initiate "top-down" programs that fail to address the very real issues and problems faced by villagers who frequently suffer loss of property or life from wild tigers. Likewise, local governments must address the quality-of-life issues of those who need and rely on the natural resources found in the tigers' territories. And finally, governments must address the health needs of their people so that the demand for tiger parts for use in traditional Chinese medicine can be eliminated. Effective and culturally acceptable medical substitutes for tiger parts, particularly bone, must be found. These might include parts harvested from cows, pigs, and other agricultural animals. Fundamental changes are also needed in the interactions between groups that work with captive and those that work with wild tigers. Those concerned with saving the tiger in the wild and those whose primary emphasis is on captive tigers must realize to a greater degree that they are working toward a common goal. Zoos are no longer simply entertainment centers but have become integral players in tiger conservation. To some degree, LSU also has a role to play in this effort, as we seek to educate our community concerning conservation issues. The great LSU tradition of Mike the Tiger has itself evolved from one of simply enhancing school spirit to participation in the noble and global effort to save one of the earth's most magnificent animals.

Tiger Traditions and Tidbits

When LSU was a military school, cadets were required to salute Mike and say, "Good morning, Mike."

The football team will score one touchdown for every time Mike roars before the game. The current tiger readily roars at the student mascot.

Mike is pulled around the stadium before each game, with the cheerleaders riding atop his trailer leading cheers.

Mike's trailer is parked next to the opposing team's locker room. When they take the field, they must run past Mike.

Until the 1970s, Mike's trailer was kept covered as he was brought into the football stadium. It

Whiskey decanter, ca. 1985.

Courtesy Karen Perronne

113

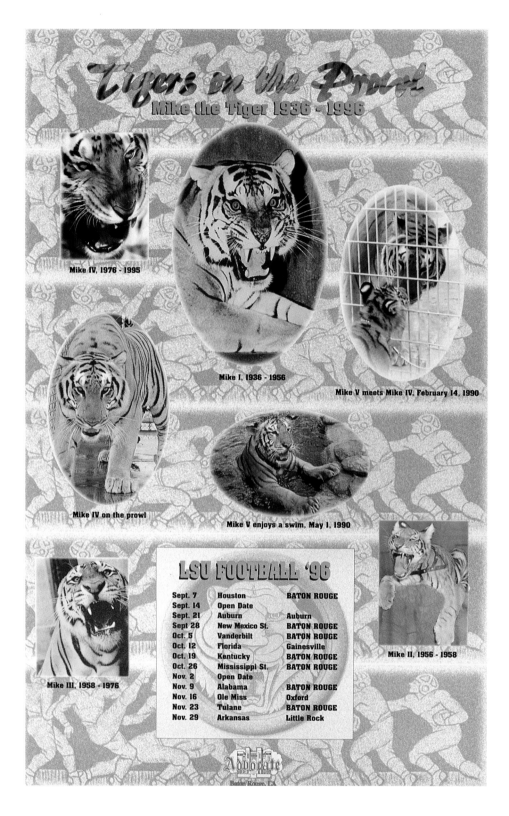

Tigers on the Prowl
Mike the Tiger 1936 - 1996

Mike IV, 1976 - 1995

Mike I, 1936 - 1956

Mike V meets Mike IV, February 14, 1990

Mike IV on the prowl

Mike V enjoys a swim, May 1, 1990

Mike III, 1958 - 1976

LSU FOOTBALL '96

Sept. 7	Houston	BATON ROUGE
Sept. 14	Open Date	
Sept. 21	Auburn	Auburn
Sept 28	New Mexico St.	BATON ROUGE
Oct. 5	Vanderbilt	BATON ROUGE
Oct. 12	Florida	Gainesville
Oct. 19	Kentucky	BATON ROUGE
Oct. 26	Mississippi St.	BATON ROUGE
Nov. 2	Open Date	
Nov. 9	Alabama	BATON ROUGE
Nov. 16	Ole Miss	Oxford
Nov. 23	Tulane	BATON ROUGE
Nov. 29	Arkansas	Little Rock

Advocate
Baton Rouge, LA

Mike II, 1956 - 1958

was uncovered, and Mike revealed, only just before kickoff. This was done to build suspense for the game and for Mike's appearance. Many years ago, Mike was prodded with a broom handle to get him to roar. Of course this is no longer allowed—nor is it necessary!

Because cats are more active at night, the football team will play better when games are scheduled at night.

SONGS

"Hey, Fightin' Tigers"

Hey, Fightin' Tigers, fight all the way.
Play, Fightin' Tigers, win the game today.
You've got the knowhow, you're doing fine.
Hang on to the ball as you hit the wall,
And smash right through the line.
You've got to go for a touchdown,
Run up the score.
Make Mike the Tiger stand right up and roar.
　　　ROAR!!!
Give it all of your might as you fight tonight,
And keep the goal in view: Victory for L-S-U!

A poster showing all of the LSU tigers through the years, produced by the Baton Rouge *Advocate* for the 1996 football season.
Courtesy Clay Stewart

114

"Tiger Rag"

Long ago, way down in the jungle
Someone got an inspiration for a tune,
And that jingle brought from the jungle
Became famous mighty soon.
Thrills and chills it sends through you!
Hot! So hot, it burns you too!
Though it's just the growl of the tiger,
It was written in a syncopated way.
More and more they howl for the Tiger,
Everywhere you go today:
They're shoutin':
Where's that Tiger! Where's that Tiger!
Where's that Tiger! Where's that Tiger!
Hold that Tiger! Hold that Tiger!
Hold that Tiger!

"The Coming of Tiger Mike"

By Marvin N. Lymberis

Come, ye children, lean this way,
And learn of the far-famed "Tiger Day."
'Twas back in the year of 'thirty-six—
    Ah, well I do remember
That the Ole War Skule made history
    On the twenty-first day of November.
The sun had not yet pierced the sky,
    When from the dead of night
The entire corps, two thousand strong,
    Made plans to greet "Tiger Mike."
A council of war was hastily called,
    And quickly did they reach

The conclusion that there could be no school
    Without any profs to teach.
So at every gate, a company formed,
    Resolved that no car should pass.
Banners were made and songs were sung,
    "No books, no profs, no class."
And when at last the mighty cat
    Did show itself on site,
The crowd went wild and cheered aloud
    For mascot "Tiger Mike."
No man or beast has e'er before
    Been greeted with such ovation—
Students, prexy, and commandment
    Joined hands in celebration.
For presidents and such may come and go,
    And their memory may die overnight,
But through the years, no one can forget
    The coming of "Tiger Mike."

This inventive mail box, an exact replica of the trailer that carries Mike, belongs to Harold Doyle Jr. of Slidell.

The living room of Drs. Jerry and Sheila Ford of Houston, Texas. Jerry Ford created much of the original artwork, such as paintings and sculptures. In the background you can see the tiger coat made especially for Sheila Ford by her mother, Mrs. Vennnie Morris.

Tommy R. Gartman

"The Bengal Bye"

A poem written in honor of Mike I
by Mr. O. C. Hupperick (The "Bengal Bard")

I recollect the day when you became
    A growing mascot of our LSU
And how you were displayed at every game
    In festive pride and with affection too.
You had a home on wheels and in a cage
    Where people visited your college sphere
Until you reached the climax of your age
    Which marked the end of your brief visit
      here.
The Reaper favors no beast or man

And so your cage becomes an empty cell;
But, "Mike," you had another home as well
    Within the heart of every loyal fan . . .
And each new team shall help exemplify
    A tiger spirit that shall never die.

QUOTES AND POEMS

General

"The tiger is a symbol of everything the university stands for. Certainly [it] is a symbol of the spirit of the university. . . . It is a rallying point everybody can identify with."
    —Sam J. Friedman (LSU Board of Supervisors, 1984–90)

"The tiger is a symbol of the university. The animal is very strong, sleek, intelligent. . . . You can perceive the university in the same way—a university which is the front line and doesn't back down to anything or anyone."
    —Dr. Jack A. Andonie (LSU Board of Supervisors)

"It seems like Mike has been that thing that somehow holds the whole university together. The tiger is a rallying point."
    —Mr. Gordon E. Doré (LSU Board of Supervisors, 1972–2000)

Mike I

"A very nice animal . . . a quiet tiger and a well-mannered one, and as far as I know, he never ate any football players."

    —Bernie Moore (head football coach, 1935–47)

"I remember it well, the day Mike came to the campus. . . . It was something. You never saw a student body react to anything like they did when Mike showed up. . . . It was a great parade, a great celebration. . . . And after that, it wasn't a football game without Mike being there. . . . He never missed a home game, and he made nearly all the road trips. Those students saw to that."

    —Bernie Moore (head football coach, 1935–47)

"Old Mike . . . he had a great career. . . . He just seemed to fit in with tradition. . . . Or maybe he became the tradition; maybe he made it what it was."

    —Bernie Moore (head football coach, 1935–47)

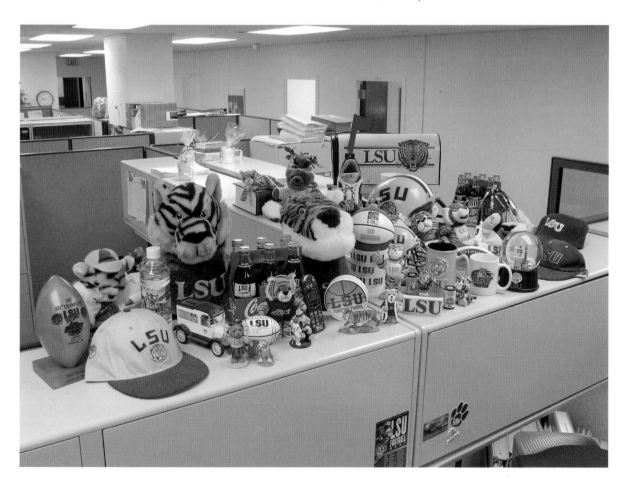

The work cubicle of Lyn Taylor sports a large array of LSU and tiger collectibles.

Prather Warren, University Relations

Auburn is the buggy,
Southwestern is the hoss,
Tulane did the driving,
For the Tigers is the boss.
— Porter "Eddie" Bryant, 1936

Mike IV:

"I see this as a once-in-a-lifetime opportunity to take care of the Bengal tiger, one experience that will be with me the rest of my life. . . . This may be the most well-known mascot in the country. . . . There is no doubt in my mind that this tiger fully represents the university to a tee."

— John DeVun (student caretaker, 1986)

"We have a funny relationship. He hates me and I respect it."

— John DeVun (student caretaker, 1986)

"The responsibility of caring for the tiger is passed on from one keeper to the next. . . . The guy before me touched me with the responsibility. I likewise will pass some of that on to the next one. I'm sure he too will pass that same tradition of responsibility to the next person after him."

— John DeVun (student caretaker, 1986)

Tiger Mardi Gras beads.

Courtesy Charles J. Becker

118

Meet me at Mike the Tiger's Cage!

Jim Zietz, University Relations

About the Photographs

All of the photographs preceding the first chapter are of Mike V and, unless otherwise indicated, were taken by C. C. Lockwood, who has generously donated his time and photographic contributions to this book. For more information on Mr. Lockwood's work, please visit www.cclockwood.com.

The painting of the *Spirit of LSU* on page 26 and the etching of Mike III on page 59 were provided free of charge for use in this book by Glenn Gore. To obtain prints of Mr. Gore's work, visit www.geocities.com/airhistory or write to OUACHITA@centurytel.net.

Many of the photographs in this book were obtained through generous donations from Mike's fans and supporters of LSU. While every effort has been made to acknowledge the donors, the source of some photographs and artifacts could not be ascertained. To all the named and unnamed contributors to this book, the publisher and the authors are sincerely grateful.